"Teall's book isn't just a riding manual—don't pick it up expecting a tutorial of how to ride a certain way, or how to put in a perfect hunter round based merely on the technical aspects. It's more of an all-over cohesive approach to riding, showing and enjoying your horse. Teall tells you to put your heels down, but he also tells you why, and how it will affect your horse, and how it will make your riding more effective. Reading and understanding Teall's logical, simple approach to the physical, technical, and—above all—mental aspects of riding will help you look at your riding in a whole new way."

—THE CHRONICLE OF THE HORSE

"If you are looking for a primer on riding hunters and equitation, you can't go wrong with this book."

—SPORT PONY

"In this elegantly illustrated book, noted judge, trainer, and clinician Geoff Teall discusses these 'basic skills'—the nuts and bolts of perfecting riding position—and demystifies the jumping course by breaking it down into simple pieces that are easily practiced at home. Teall also helps readers examine their short- and long-term goals and devise a tailor-made plan to achieve them while enjoying horses and riding along the way."

—EQUINE JOURNAL

GEOFF TEALL

On Riding Hunters, Jumpers and Equitation

GEOFF TEALL
On Riding Hunters, Jumpers and Equitation

DEVELOP A WINNING STYLE

Geoff Teall

with
AMI HENDRICKSON

Foreword by
CARLETON BROOKS
Note to the Reader by
PIPER KLEMM, PhD

TRAFALGAR SQUARE
North Pomfret, Vermont

First published in 2006 by
Trafalgar Square Books
North Pomfret, Vermont 05053

Reprint 2020

Library of Congress Cataloging-in-Publication Data

Teall, Geoff.
  Geoff teall on riding hunters, jumpers and equitation: develop a winning style / Geoff Teall with Ami Hendrickson.
    p. cm.
  Includes index.
  ISBN-13: 978-1-57076-333-5 (hardcover)
  ISBN-10: 1-57076-333-X (hardcover)
  ISBN-13: 978-1-57076-344-1 (paperback)
  ISBN-10: 1-57076-344-5 (paperback)
  1. Hunt riding. 2. Jumping (Horsemanship) 3. Show jumping. 4. Hunter seat equitation.
  I. Hendrickson, Ami. II. Title.
  SF295.65.T43 2006
  798.2—dc22
                                    2005035321

Illustration credits:
Photos: Diana De Rosa (pages 7, 8, 14, 19, 24, 27, 30, 33, 38, 41, 45–6, 51, 53–4, 59–62, 66–70, 74–6, 79, 82 *left*, 85, 90–2, 94, 102, 104, 153, 156, 163, 173–4, 175 *bottom*, 182, 185, 189, 205, 220, 235–6, 239, 244, 247, 252); Miranda Lorraine (pages 2, 6, 10, 13, 47, 78, 89, 97, 99, 101, 103, 105, 108–13, 115–8, 121–2, 124–6, 128–35, 137, 143–4, 147–8, 150–1, 154–5, 157–9, 161, 164, 167, 175 *top*, 176, 180, 183, 193–5, 199, 200, 202–3, 211, 214, 221, 225, 227, 229, 240); Ray Orth (pages 3, 11, 40, 77, 82 *right*); Charles Hilton (pages 23, 26); Randy Muster (page 56). *Illustrations:* Heidi Scheing.

Book design by Carrie Fradkin
Cover design by RM Didier
Typeface: Minion, Albertan LTL

Printed in China

10 9 8 7 6 5 4 3 2 1

WARNING

Equine riding and training can be a hazardous activity that may subject participants to possible serious injury. Geoff Teall, Ami Hendrickson, Trafalgar Square Books, and their associates will not assume any liability for your activities.

This book provides general information, instructions, and techniques that may not be suitable for everyone. No warranty is given regarding the suitability of this information, the instructions, and techniques to you or other individuals acting under your directions. Qualified personal instruction is suggested to best understand the ideas presented in this volume.

To Mike Kelly for showing me the path,

and to my parents, George and Eleanore Teall, for allowing me to follow it.

Contents

Foreword
Carleton Brooks

I HAVE A GREAT RESPECT for Geoff Teall, and we share a lot of the same ideals when it comes to horses and riding. As Geoff writes in this very book: "Desire, interest, and commitment are the most important contributors to a winning ride." I wholeheartedly agree.

But before you can win, you have to learn. The best horse people are the ones who love learning—and who never stop learning. The day you stop learning is the day you stop progressing in this sport.

So, to all the horsemen and horsewomen out there who want to learn, allow me to put it quite simply: You should fill up your notebook while reading this book. Reading and note-taking are so important to being a good horse person. I'd even call them critical. I have countless notebooks myself, and I encourage anyone reading *Geoff Teall on Riding Hunters, Jumpers and Equitation* to start their own collection as well. Applying Geoff's knowledge and instruction to your horse and your riding is how you'll get the most out of this book.

To be a good student of the sport, and a good client wherever you ride, you'll want to find a good system for yourself and your horse. That requires you to do your research on barns and trainers in order to make an educated decision. Everyone has their own system, and there are plenty of variations. But as long as your animal is in an environment that puts the horses first, you've made a solid first step. Then, it's up to you to patiently trust the system.

Geoff and I both turned our focus to education later in our careers. My wife Traci and I started Balmoral TV, and Geoff brought this book into the world. I am so pleased that it's available in print again. I hope that you soak up everything that it has to teach you.

Keep learning. Keep progressing.

Carleton Brooks
Balmoral Farm
Inducted National Show Hunter Hall of Fame, 2019
USEF "R" Judge since 1985

Note to the Reader
Piper Klemm

GROWING UP AS A HORSE ENTHUSIAST, I checked out every single book about horses from my local library—most of them many times. I read every second that I couldn't be at the barn learning horsemanship hands-on. My own riding career had its ups and downs, but my background consuming equine knowledge and my love of horses led to me eventually publishing *The Plaid Horse*.

When I started teaching college equestrian courses, I sat down with all the resources our market had to offer and was happily surprised by the wealth of information that has come out in the last twenty years. Upon reading and reflecting on all of these books, the standout text was clearly *Geoff Teall on Riding Hunters, Jumpers and Equitation*.

Geoff Teall on Riding Hunters, Jumpers and Equitation is the fundamental primer that I hope every English rider or aspiring rider takes the time to read thoroughly. And I hope they will re-read it every few years, applying their own enhanced experiences and perspectives to each reading. For the seasoned rider, it is such a thoughtful and clear take on the fundamentals, which often are sadly lost in our fast-paced and overly horse-show-centric environment. The book impressed me so much that *The Plaid Horse* wanted to be a part of its new life with a new printing in order to get it into as many equestrians' hands as possible. Geoff's work remains as strong and relevant as ever. As much as things have changed in our sport, so much about riding hunters, jumpers, and equitation has not. "Classic" still wins in the show ring.

Riders can take responsibility for so many aspects of this sport: their discipline, their preparation, the goals they are trying to achieve, and their mental game. Geoff goes through every facet of both technical riding and how to navigate the world of hunters, jumpers, and equitation for the best results possible. He discusses listening to the horse; training and care in a no-frills, horse-centered mentality; and the steps individuals must take to have opportunities opened up to them. His discussions on getting help, undermounting yourself, and setting appropriate goals are frank, coherent, and straightforward.

Good fundamentals take so long to learn, but they are the only approach for long-term success in the equestrian industry. While gimmicks and shortcuts can seem to be all the rage, they always end up falling short, left in the dust over time by the earnings and winnings of true horse people. In this book and in person, Geoff evangelizes the horse's well-being and safety over winning, taking the time to train both horse and rider properly before competition, and putting a lifelong riding career over a single goal.

It's been a privilege to teach equestrian college courses and to help educate people in our sport through *The Plaid Horse*. Reminding riders how much they do have within their control in this sport is a prompting we all need, and Geoff's forthright discussions help people make better observations at every level.

In the pages that follow, Geoff clearly lays out how to grow your mastery of this sport and all it entails, from mental game, to appropriate goals, to enjoying your animals. We hope you enjoy reading this superb book.

Piper Klemm
Publisher, *The Plaid Horse*
Professor of Sports Studies
Host of *The #Plaidcast*
Author of *Show Strides*

An Introduction to Balanced Riding

A Definition of Terms

This is a book about riding.

It is about riding in the most correct, skilled, beautiful, and balanced way possible. It is about understanding the merits of fundamental horsemanship principles and applying them to your efforts. It is about knowing what you want to do with your riding and equipping yourself for success.

For many, good riding that is correct in both form and function is synonymous with *equitation*. But talking about equitation can be a tricky business.

In the hunter world, Hunt Seat Equitation is a competitive division. With a few exceptions, that division is open primarily to junior riders. It is intended to make riders aware of good position and to create a solid foundation built on strong basic skills.

The annual Hunt Seat Equitation Finals are the pinnacle of the division. Here the most correct, most polished, and most accomplished riders shine.

In hunt seat circles, finals winners are a very big deal. They often go on to enjoy lengthy, successful careers hunting, jumping, or eventing. But then, so do those who begin riding too late in life to compete in equitation classes—which brings me to the larger definition of the term.

I see equitation as more than just a division of competition dedicated to making young riders into good riders.

To me, equitation is a means to an end. The word literally means "the art of riding on horseback." It encompasses the concepts of horsemanship, correctness of position, and riding skills.

The rider who applies the basic principles of equitation hones his skills and develops the tools he will need for a lifetime with horses.

My entire approach to training effective riders is built on this philosophy. I believe that an understanding and a mastery of sound riding principles gives the hunt seat rider the skills needed to succeed in all facets of riding including jumping, dressage, showing hunters, fox hunting, or pleasure riding.

1.1 *"Equitation" denotes an approach to riding, and to horses in general, that focuses on balance, control, harmony, and grace.*

1.2 *A sound equitation foundation will allow you to succeed in any riding endeavor.*

The Benefits of Equitation

A thorough understanding of the fundamentals of good horsemanship benefits the rider in many ways. As a rider, perfecting your form and position provides you with a wealth of skills that will help you cope with the problems and difficult situations you will surely encounter in your riding career.

Equitation work stretches you. Equitation riders learn more about lengthening and shortening, turning, lightening, and making their horses responsive than most riders in other disciplines.

Since fine-tuning your equitation skills involves learning how to ride into and out of specific problems, you learn a lot about training. Not only do you learn how to train yourself to jump with fluidity, style, and grace, but you also learn how to train your horse to do the same.

The Equitation Foundation

When equitation is done well, it creates a solid riding foundation. It will help you understand sound training principles. An equitation background has the potential to give you a wonderfully broad base for your riding.

Focusing on your form, your balance, and your position will improve your riding in other areas. It can help polish you as a spectacular hunter rider. Your training will make your style greater, which will dress up any horse you ride.

Perfecting your position, your poise, and your timing can help make you a great jumper rider because your basic skills will be grounded in efficiency. You will also have gained invaluable experience in training horses and in making them rideable.

The Larger Picture

Many benefits may be gained from concentrating on perfecting your equitation—and not all of them have to do with better riding.

Equitation work takes discipline. It improves your time management skills. It teaches you to control your attitude and your outlook. It strengthens your coordination and gives you experience in getting along with both people and animals.

In many respects, just about all of life's lessons—anything you need to know in order to deal with people in the "real world"—will be learned from working with horses, trainers, and fellow competitors.

Why Ride?
Motivators and Philosophy

The Classic Approach

"Classic," to me, means using time-proven methods. The study of horses and riding has been around for centuries. Good, solid, classic training principles are based on horses' consistent reactions to various stimuli. These reactions are the same now as they were hundreds of years ago (figs. 2.1 A & B).

Since horses have not changed over the centuries, there is much to be gained from studying and emulating the training techniques that achieved results long ago. I don't believe that training techniques need to change to fit our "modern" sensibilities. It isn't necessary to reinvent the wheel in horse training. It is far better, in my opinion, to study the masters that have come before us and do our best to learn from them.

I believe that all training solutions are out there. It is our job as riders to learn them and discover how to best use them.

Classics in a Modern Age

A traditional approach to riding is no less applicable now than it was several hundred years ago. Such an approach has great value in the twenty-first century. As time goes by, and horses are no longer an essential part of daily life, we run the very real danger of losing the knowledge that was once commonplace.

The more horses become luxuries rather than necessities, the more it is imperative that we learn as many time-tested techniques as possible. I believe

2.1 A *If you close your leg on a horse, he will react by moving forward.*

B *If done properly, closing your fingers on the reins will cause him to slow down.*

an understanding of these techniques is critical to effectively communicating with the modern horse.

In with the Old; Out with the New

By nature, I am suspicious of "new." I prefer tried and true. I prefer to stay with proven practices that I know work. If something has been effective for the past generation, and the one before that and—in all probability—the one before *that*, then I can reasonably assume that it will work for me as well.

In my experience, people will try something "new" in training because they believe there is a substitute for good, old-fashioned, hard work. They will go all the way down the road on that new approach, only to discover that it doesn't work for various reasons. Very often, those people will then set about looking for another quick fix—which doesn't exist.

An understanding of the physics of riding tells me that if I ride a horse in a particular way, and I do a particular thing with my hands and my legs, then I will get a particular result. To my mind, there is no need to look for new ways to accomplish the same things I can using tried and true techniques.

"New" ways tend to be more complicated. By definition, they are unproven. They often involve gimmicks and equipment to *force* the horse to do something rather than *train* him to do it. For these reasons, I believe they are generally inferior to traditional methodology.

The Form of Function

Correct equitation is all about style. It is about function. It is the form that follows function (fig. 2.2).

It often seems that people are too quick to let go of things that are a little difficult to attain. Riding a horse invisibly, in a beautiful, solid position, with

2.2 *Equitation evolved as a form for a specific function. Here, the rider is correct and accurate in her position. She has independent hands and an independent seat. She is a secure rider, but at the same time, she's relaxed. This allows her horse to be relaxed and working forward. The rider's balance and position enhance the horse's performance.*

sound, deliberate training techniques has never been—and never will be— easy. But it is better than the sloppy, rough, haphazard alternatives.

Throughout the years, man has learned where to sit on the horse for the best balance and control. He has discovered how to get the horse to react in

2.3 *Equitation as a discipline doesn't exist because it makes the rider look pretty on the horse. Instead, the rider looks good because a correct position allows the horse to move to the best of his ability.*

a certain way. But man did not invent these training principles. The horses themselves have taught us the methods that work consistently.

Getting a desired response from the animal is the reason for riding him in a particular way. And, since horses don't react any differently to stimuli now than they did hundreds of years ago, the time-honored approach simply makes sense.

It is critical that we don't lower our standards to focus only on form or on function. An appreciation of both is needed for effective riding. A good rider, regardless of his riding discipline, needs good position. He also needs to be able, within that good position, to perform his function. One helps the other. High standards for both are essential.

Equitation as Art

There is an art to riding the horse. The art is in doing *just enough* with the training and doing *just enough* when you ride. A great rider is subtle in his movements. To any onlooker, it is not obvious what the rider is doing to make the horse respond. The point, in the end, is invisible aids.

Much riding today is nothing more than "Hollywood on horseback." It is concerned with whether or not the riders are wearing the latest apparel. It is obsessed with how the horses look. It is all about long tails and current fashion. But, these surface aspects are not the foundation of good riding.

As a rider and competitor, I want my horse to be in top shape and well

---

JUDGE'S CARD
FORM AND FUNCTION

Which should take precedence: form or function?

In other words, should you ride in a correct position, knowing your horse might not have the training or the talent to respond correctly? Or, should you sacrifice position to make sure that the horse gets the job done? When you are not yet competing at the top levels, this can be a real dilemma.

This topic is a tricky part of judging. As a judge, my instinct is to favor function over form, if I *must* choose. But, it often depends on the individual riders in the class in question.

When I have a hard time deciding where I will lower my standards (as when pinning a lower-level equitation class), I consider everything in relation to the horse. Let's say I must choose between two contestants:

- One rider has excellent position but is stiff as a board and consequently annoys and bothers the horse.
- The other rider has poorer position but is going with the flow and not irritating the horse.

I would let the horse be the deciding factor in this situation. I would pin the rider who is less offensive to the horse. To me, the horse is the best judge of a rider's ability.

The ideal I am always looking for, however, is the rider with good style who isn't so stiff and artificial that he affects the horse in an unnatural way.

---

groomed. Beyond that, however, cosmetics are unimportant. I am much more interested in my horse's performance—and my own. Great performances come from great position.

The Classic Position

Over the hundreds of years that we have been training horses and riders, the ideal position of the rider on the horse has evolved (fig. 2.4).

"Correct" or "classic" position depends entirely upon the purpose of the ride. The proper position for a rider of classical dressage, for instance, is not the optimum classic position for a hunter or a jumper. Riding over fences depends on a position more suited for following, rather than influencing the horse (for more on riding to follow or to influence, see p. 122). Therefore, the proper, "classic" jumping position is a considerably more forward one, with the angles

2.4 The classic hunt seat, or forward seat position on horseback is a perfect blend of form and function. Everything about it serves a purpose.

of the rider's knees, hips, and elbows more pronounced than in classical dressage.

The correct position involves the rider sitting straight in the saddle with his legs stretched long and around the horse. The heels are down as deeply as possible to lower the rider's center of gravity and improve stability.

The stomach and rib cage are lifted up a bit, improving the rider's posture and giving a slight arch to the back.

The arms are soft and elastic, forming a straight line from the elbow to the bit. They allow the horse to be ridden with contact without putting pressure on the bars of the mouth.

The rider's head is up and his eyes are looking ahead—further improving his balance and synchronicity with the horse. (For a more in-depth look at the various aspects of position, see chapter 9, *Perfect Position: Understanding and Developing the Physical Aids*.)

Correct position was created out of necessity. It is the easiest way to hold your balance and maintain your security on the horse. At the same time, it allows you to effectively communicate your wants and needs to the horse.

Good horsemanship is about being in a position where you can best influence your horse. The rider's goal—the purpose of perfecting your position—is riding with independent hands and an independent seat.

Independent hands mean you do not rely on your hands for balance. You do not clutch at the reins to keep you on the horse. Independent hands allow you to relate to the horse's mouth, head, and neck in specific ways. They guide the horse, but do not randomly interfere with him.

An independent seat means that you use only your leg and your base for balance and security on the horse. Obviously, being in the middle of the horse's back, being secure in the saddle, being balanced, and being confident will help all of your riding—whether you ultimately want to ride jumpers or hunters, ride cross-country, go trail riding, or ride to hounds.

Keep It Simple

Riding isn't complicated. It isn't easy, either. It is a discipline that requires you to work hard at perfecting the basics, even though the "basics" are simple to understand. Keep your heels down. Establish an even pace. Maintain steady contact. These are not complicated concepts, but they can take a long time to master.

In the same vein, holding the reins isn't physically difficult (it is quite simple, really), but you must hone the skills required so the reins feel natural in your hands rather than awkward.

The best rider is not great because he does all sorts of complicated or difficult moves on the horse. He isn't the one who does bizarre, outrageous, obvious, or esoteric things.

The best rider is the one who does the simplest, most classic, most artful pieces of riding better than anybody else. His leg position is better than anybody else's, and so is the position of his hands and his arms. His discipline, cleanliness, and timeliness are better. He excels in the simple things, and that gives him the foundation for greatness.

2.5 *You want to be as much a part of the horse as possible so the two of you are better able to do interesting things together.*

No One Said It Would Be Easy

I don't believe the correct position is "easy." In fact, when you begin riding it is easier to let your leg and heel come up and to allow your upper body to collapse forward.

It is better, however, if you can keep your weight down in your leg and stretch your legs so they are as long as possible. This ultimately offers a more secure seat and gives you better communication with the horse.

Similarly, it is not easier—but it is better—to hold your upper body straight and strong, while your hands and your arms stay supple. Correct body position gives you strength, security, and balance. At the same time, soft arms and hands allow for good communication through the bit.

An independent seat and independent hands are not easy to develop—but they are necessary. Though classically beautiful equitation is an "art," every piece of the art form was developed for a reason.

Time has shown us where to be on the horse, in relation to the horse's build and balance, in order to be the most effective. The fact that it is physically demanding to get there and the fact that it goes against your first instinct doesn't matter. The fact that *it works* is what makes it both important and necessary. Therefore, in order to ride well, you need to work hard enough to master the physical demands of correct position.

Mastering the principles of good equitation gives you a tremendous sense of pride and respect. The respect is not only for yourself and for the horse, but for the sport of riding as well.

Building a Solid Foundation

As you learn to ride, if you take enough time to build your foundation of good position, solid riding skills, and basic training skills, you will end up reaching your end goals faster.

The Fast Way Is the Slow Way

Riding is a bit like the old fable of the tortoise and the hare: slow and steady wins out in the end.

I often caution my overly ambitious students about cutting corners. "The fast way is the slow way," I warn them.

If you skip things in the beginning, or try to move up through the divisions too quickly, you may start out ahead of the others. But, you will inevitably end up backsliding, and you will have to backtrack to learn the parts you missed. You will ultimately spend more time unlearning bad habits and forming good ones than you would have spent learning the good habits to begin with.

Equitation is about mastering the pieces of riding and then putting those pieces together in a unified, effective whole. The whole process takes time.

A Talent for Riding

I think it is easy for students (myself included) to use "lack of talent" as a way to avoid working too hard. Lack of talent is a great stress reliever. It allows you to say things like, "I didn't do that right. It's not because I am not trying hard; it's because I'm not talented."

What a ridiculous excuse!

Talent is *so* unimportant when compared to interest, when compared to desire, and when compared to hard work. It is a very, very small piece of the puzzle.

To my mind, a disciplined rider of lesser talent will always shine above the undisciplined, talented rider. In this sport, drive and determination are enormously leveling factors.

Work with What You Have

Physical attributes can help your riding, but they are not necessary. The ideal rider has long legs, a short body, and long arms. That is the easiest type of anatomy to work with.

The more you are restricted by your physical size and shape, the more difficult it may be for you to excel. But, even if you are not the ideal body type, take heart. In my experience, good equitation is never impossible.

A good rider needs a good brain. He needs to be relaxed, interested, determined, disciplined, and strong. In many ways, these attributes take precedence over a rider's physical characteristics.

I really stress with my riders who are not tall or thin (the aesthetically ideal body type) that riding is a *sport*. The more you regulate your weight and control it, the more you keep yourself fit and strong, the easier riding will be. Riding can be used to help you get in shape. If riding doesn't come naturally or easily to you, it will still help you develop physical strength, fitness, and control over your body.

The more your age, weight, coordination, or conformation hinders your progress, the more you have to rely on a solid foundation. The most basic part of your foundation of course, is solid position.

Make yourself repeatedly go back and regroup as you practice the basics. Then practice them some more, until you have such a sound, solid foundation that you are secure, comfortable, and as knowledgeable as you can be on the horse.

2.6 *In riding, everything big relates to something small. You can't have good position without a good leg. You can't have a good leg without correctly placing your foot in the iron.*

2.7 Interest is the most important factor in your riding ability. This older, experienced student's interest in correct position and perfecting her craft shows in her schooling.

The less raw talent you possess, the more you need to rely on a slow and steady approach to learning how to ride. Do it for the process rather than for the results. And, bear in mind that success is measured in many different ways.

Riding should never be discouraging for you if you are not the "right size" or the "right shape." The important things are desire and drive and ambition. Don't despair. Just get to work and get things done.

Start at the beginning. Start with your leg and work your way up. Continually strive to perfect the correct position.

Work on your abilities one step at a time and methodically learn how to ride. Then, methodically teach your horse how to do his job.

The better your foundation, and the more skills you can master, the better you will be able to deal with the day-to-day challenges that arise. You will also find that once you have the basics mastered, your riding will improve exponentially and you and your horse will be much more of a team.

Focus on Causes Rather than Symptoms

Regardless of how much talent or ability you may possess, no horse or rider is perfect. When a problem arises—and it will—it helps to have a methodical approach to solving it.

To discover the underlying problem, you have to take an unemotional moment to analyze the symptoms you don't like. Decide, first of all, if something is a symptom, or if it is a problem in and of itself.

If you don't accurately diagnose the problem, you will waste your energies on tangents. This happens all the time at horse shows. People who are going too slowly work on straightening instead of pace. People who are nervous work on pace rather than trying to calm themselves. All of their hard work is for nothing because it does not begin to fix their fundamental problems.

Problem solving is one reason why it is important to surround yourself with knowledgeable, competent horse people. Use their expertise to help you develop the art of looking at a situation and identifying the problems that exist.

Once the problems have been identified, it is important to choose the one that is the most pertinent at that moment. After isolating the core problem, then you can come up with simple, unemotional solutions to fix it.

If things go wrong and the rider freaks out over a symptom, riding becomes nerve-wracking. It becomes conflicting, uncomfortable, and worrisome for both horse and rider, because focusing on a symptom will *never* correct the underlying cause of the trouble.

When a problem manifests itself, you have to stop. Remove any emotion you bring to the situation. Look for the root cause; then decide what you will do to solve the problem.

Instinctive Riding

As a rider, give yourself credit for being aware of your horse. Instead of second-guessing yourself, pay attention to your instinct. For instance:

- If you think your pace is too slow—it probably is.
- If you think your horse is dead to your legs—he probably is.
- If you think your horse has a dead mouth—he probably does.
- If you think your horse is moving stiffly or feels lame—he probably is.
- If you don't think your horse is reacting correctly—he probably isn't.

If, in your riding, something "just doesn't feel right," don't be in a hurry to discount it or ignore it. Riding is a tactile, physical exercise that relies at least as much on feel as it does on logic.

"Feeling" often alerts you to problems with your horse, with a course, or with your riding. Once the problems are defined, however, logic helps you solve them.

Watch for "Tack-Masking"

In many ways, riding emulates life. There are no shortcuts to success. Quick fixes and easy cures rarely exist.

Consider your tack, for instance. If you discover that using a particular piece of equipment improves your riding or your horse's way of going, use it for a while if you must. However, don't stop there. Apply yourself to determining what caused the improvement. Ask yourself what underlying weakness in structure, experience, or schooling the new equipment is masking. Then work on devising a way to strengthen the inherent weakness, rather than simply patching it.

If you can fix the problem, then, when it is gone, the symptoms of that problem will also disappear. You will have spent your energies getting to the root of the matter, rather than trying to mask or cover one piece of the larger puzzle.

Let's apply the principle of focusing on causes rather than symptoms to two cases—one where the underlying problem lies with the horse, and one where the problem is the rider's fault:

Case Study 1: The Heavy Horse

If your horse is heavy and dead to your hands, his lowness, heaviness, and unresponsiveness are all *symptoms*. The underlying *cause*, in many cases, is a lack of balance.

If your horse isn't correctly balanced, he isn't using his hind end properly. Rather than being balanced over his haunches and using the hindquarters for impulsion, his hind end trails behind him. Therefore, leaning on your hands is the only way he can balance himself.

For many, the quick fix in this case would be to use a stronger bit, such as a gag bit or a Pelham, that would allow the rider to forcibly lift the horse's head up while riding the horse forward.

If the problem stems from the horse's hind end, however, trying to fix it from the front (using more bit) isn't going to help. Pulling the horse's head up won't make him lighter in your hands. It also won't be effective in teaching him to balance himself.

Instead of focusing on the symptom of heaviness, you must address the cause if you are to make a permanent change.

In order to use his hind end for forward impulsion, the horse has to become responsive to your legs. He should move forward from your leg. He should use his hind end to balance himself. Only then will he be able to respond to your hands and get light with his front end.

All the bits in the world won't make an unbalanced horse move correctly. The best they will do is mask the problem for a time. But, you can use the art of riding—your equitation—to affect your horse's way of going. Exercises that target the cause of the problem, rather than the symptoms, will result in a horse that moves and responds correctly without relying on equipment for his balance.

Two exercises that are good for improving a horse's ability to work off his hindquarters are "Push, Don't Pull" (see p. 148) and "Trot a Round" (see p. 226). Working the horse on these and similar lessons will help correct the root cause of his heaviness. It will enable him to be better balanced and to carry himself properly. Then, there should be no reason to mask the problem with harsher tack.

Case Study 2: Chipping

Focusing on symptoms rather than causes is also easy to do when it comes to the rider's performance.

A common example in the show ring is "chipping," or going for a long distance, missing it, and adding a short stride just before the fence. As the rider makes his round, the horse is missing his distances and chipping all over the ring. When this happens, the rider often focuses on the fact that he is chipping, rather than realizing why.

One root problem of chipping could be very simple: not enough pace. If you are working under the pace needed for the course, chipping is a common symptom. To fix the problem, instead of worrying about missing the distance to the fence, simply pick up the pace to the point where the horse is able to perform better.

Another, more complex problem, could be nerves. If you never chip when practicing at home but always do at a horse show, perhaps your environment makes the difference.

If nerves are the problem, work on getting your emotions under better control (for more on managing nervousness, see "Fighting Stage Fright, Nerves, and Other Bogeymen," p. 81). As you gain more confidence and experience, the chipping will disappear.

Stay Cool

Lack of emotion is the key to seeing beyond symptoms to the underlying cause of a problem.

When trying to get to the bottom of something, choose a moment when you are not emotionally involved with what is going wrong. Don't hesitate to talk with someone who is educated and uninvolved (or at least less invested in the problem than you are). Ask questions. Don't be too proud to ask for help to find your solution.

Keeping a cool head is a component of a balanced approach. When talking about the art of equitation, a basic assumption is that you do not allow negative emotions to color your riding.

We have all seen it: for some reason, be it a lack of training, bad footing, or sloppy riding, a horse performs poorly and the rider takes it personally. As the rider rants, the horse invariably reacts negatively—and the drama escalates.

Anytime emotion enters into your schooling or training program, you inevitably make errors in judgment. If you allow emotions to affect your actions, your horse is the one who suffers.

If you ever find yourself feeling angry or upset, or if you feel the urge to strong-arm your horse and ride roughly, stop. Quit whatever it is you're doing. Clear your head. Take a break. You might even need to dismount and put the horse away.

Don't allow riding to get to be "Too Much." It should never put so much pressure on you or have so much significance that it is no longer enjoyable. If you feel that your riding has crossed the "Too Much" line, stop and do something else. Give yourself a chance to settle down before you try again.

Horses do not understand emotional reactions, but they have incredible memories. Distance yourself from the situation if your emotional state makes it necessary. Then come back and try again when you are in better control of yourself.

Less Is More

Look for ways to achieve your end goals while doing less.

Whenever possible, try to subtract something from the whole. Always be on the lookout for a way to do more with less. You might take something away from your tack, your schooling work, or your jumps. You may enter fewer classes at a show. The simpler you can keep your riding, the stronger it will be.

Less jumping, less drilling, less ringwork, and less fuss will only improve your horse's soundness, willingness, and attitude toward his job.

Replace Time with Training

I once had a horse that jumped well sent to me. The people who had the horse before just couldn't get him quiet.

If he was a little fresh, they would work him a little bit more. If he was still fresh, they would do still more. Eventually, the horse required so much work that they just couldn't give him any more—and he still wasn't quiet.

My ultimate goal with that horse was to have consistent performance without a huge allotment of warm-up time. I wanted to replace time with training. To that end, instead of adding more and more work and trying to get the horse quiet all the time, I decreased his work time and did not make it contingent on his performance.

2.8 *Although my horse is only playing, I would have preferred he waited to do so after we exited the show ring. However, I just let him express himself and continue with our ride. When the unexpected occurs, do not allow negative emotions to color your riding. Keep a cool head.*

10 WAYS TO KEEP YOUR COOL

1 Pet your horse.
   (Petting doesn't do a
   thing for the horse's
   nerves, but it can do
   wonders to relax the
   rider.)
2 Tell jokes.
3 Take a rest.
4 Eat lunch.
5 Don't ride that horse
   for a few days.
6 Ride another horse.
7 Have somebody else
   ride your horse.
8 Dismount and take a
   walk.
9 Muck stalls.
10 Take a shower.

The first day I rode the horse, he was wild the whole time. At the end of twenty minutes, I got off.

The next day I rode him for twenty minutes. He was wild. I got off.

I did the same thing for two or three weeks. Whether he was wild or whether he was quiet, it didn't make any difference: I rode that horse for twenty minutes, regardless.

After a while, he got used to only doing twenty minutes of work. He gave up being crazy because he knew the end of the session was never far away. Soon, the biggest problem I had with him was trying to keep him from getting *too* quiet.

When we eventually sold him, he was very quiet and very easy to ride. He still is.

Too often, people add stronger bits, more time, more work, and more gimmicks to a horse's training until they finally run out of time, work, gimmicks, and tack. Then the horse is declared "no good" and that is the end of the story.

Some people believe that, over time, horses become more and more difficult to train. I think that the reverse is true. If you school a horse and work with him properly, training him should get progressively easier.

"Subtract" Tack after Training

The "less is more" concept also applies to the tack you use.

For example, consider bitting options. During the course of training, people often progress to harsher and harsher bits, citing a need for more control of the horse.

In reality, the primary reasons to progress to a harsher bit are poor hands and a lack of training. Rather than increasing bit severity, look for ways to perfect your riding and improve your horse's training so that you can ride him in bits that are less and less severe.

The only time you should use a stronger bit is when it is necessary to get the reaction you want so can you teach the horse. As soon as the horse learns, however, go back to a lesser bit.

Make a Difference for the Better

All of your training should make a difference for the better. The most consistent practice schedule won't do any good if your riding makes your horse stiff, sore, and uncomfortable.

Your goal when riding is to teach your horse to be relaxed and supple. Then his job gets easier. He can become more and more responsive to you.

When the horse understands what you want from him, there is no need to drill endlessly. Riding well is all about subtracting the unnecessary parts and focusing on what is *needed*.

Consider your schooling time. If you generally ride for an hour, analyze what you want to accomplish in that time. Then, see if you can get it done just as effectively in forty-five minutes. Once that is possible, work at decreasing your schooling time to just half an hour. Make every minute count—then stop.

Beware of saying, "I'll do a little bit more *just in case*." That means you are making the horse do more work because of your uncertainty. The overall principle of good horsemanship, and the art of riding, is to ride with as little exertion as possible.

As a general rule, I try to get my riders and students to do the least amount of schooling necessary. I like to put my horses to bed the night before the show ready to go. Then, I only need to do some quick longeing or flatwork in the morning to fine tune them before I send them into the show ring.

When schooling, continually remind yourself that less is more. If you can get a perfect jump after ten schooling jumps, try to do it in nine. Then do it in seven. Then four. Look for ways to reward yourself and your horse for mastering something, rather than repeating it until it becomes monotonous, mechanical, and dull.

Worthwhile Warm-Ups

The warm-up is just a limbering-up time. It is not a punishment for being fresh. It is not time for training. It is not time for re-training. Most people warm up for the ring more than they need to.

By the time you get to the horse show, your skills are set for that event. You will not magically master some new part of riding in the warm-up ring. Use the warm-up to practice a little of one thing or another. Then go into the ring and do what you went there to do.

Some people think they need to jump a lot of warm-up jumps. They will start with a lot of low ones. Then, they will do some medium ones—and then they will jump some high ones. In my experience, this is a waste of the rider's time and the horse's attitude.

If your horse knows what is expected of him, he doesn't need a lot of warming up. He can do a few fences to get a feel for the venue, and then he is ready to do his job. So few people understand this. Unfortunately, their horses are the ones who suffer because of it.

The classes at most larger horse shows start on Wednesday. The warm-up classes are generally on Tuesday. It is not uncommon to see people in the schooling area warming up over the schooling jumps for hours before they go into the ring—where they will warm up some more before jumping a course.

I don't do that. I jump one warm-up jump in the ring. And, then I do the course. If the horse is in shape and knows what he is doing, he doesn't need more than that.

I save about thirty jumps just by not warming up for the warm-up. That's thirty fewer takeoffs and landings on my horse's legs. My horse isn't "warmed" into a coma, and I have still accomplished my goal, which is to show the horse the arena and school over the show's jumps.

Don't Forget Downtime

The "less is more" philosophy is a tremendously important part of what I do. I really believe that we are too quick to humanize horses and assign our values to them. At the end of the day, we like to have a nice shower and get cleaned up. I am not at all sure that horses do.

I am quite sure that they *don't* like braiding and pulling and twitching and trimming and all of that nonsense. I think horses would much rather lounge around in their pajamas with their socks half off.

I try to consciously create "downtime" for my horses. I like to pull their shoes and let their manes and coats grow. I like to let them get dirty. For some time every year, my horses live like…horses. I believe that this downtime is good for their bodies and their brains.

If I had to give just one word of advice for improving your horse's life, it would be "Stop."

Stop picking at him. Stop clutching the reins. Stop smothering him. Stop fussing. Just stop.

Horses don't like fluffy boots. They don't like lengthy bubble baths. They don't like being brushed and braided and primped and polished all the time.

They don't like wearing clothes.

Horses like wide open spaces with a little dirt, a little water, and lots of grass. They like being left alone to eat and socialize with other horses.

I am not suggesting that you stop spending time with your horse. But make the time that you spend with him count for something.

Improve your riding so you are capable of telling the horse what you want from him. Be clear and specific. Let him give you what you want in small pieces. Reward him when he is done. For a horse, the best reward is just backing off and giving him some downtime. It improves his learning curve faster than anything else.

Make the most of your time on the horse and in the saddle. Get rid of the "time-wasters." You and your horse will both benefit from a more focused approach to your training.

Getting "The Point"

So what, then, is "the point" of equitation?

It is to ride your horse invisibly. It is to have a horse that is responsive to your training, and to hone your riding skills, and continuously improve on them.

2.9 *No work for a period of time makes the horse more willing the rest of the year.*

As an instructor, my goal is to create riders who are self-sufficient. I want them to eventually be able to go off on their own and be able to really *ride*. I want them to be secure, safe, confident, and skilled. I want them to train with and learn from other people. I want them to be able to train horses and—hopefully—teach others. I always teach my students as if they will one day become teachers themselves.

2.10 *In the end, it is all about spending quality time with your horse.*

Many of my equitation students continue to develop their riding careers. I love to see my riders years after they have left my instruction and continued their schooling. Knowing that they were not only able to add to what they learned with me but were also motivated enough and interested enough to search for more knowledge gives me great satisfaction.

The point of equitation, to me, is to keep the common sense approach to good horsemanship alive and well. It is about continually striving to perfect the art while thoroughly enjoying the sport.

3

Instruction Matters

Assembling Your Riding Team

Riding instruction is tremendously important. I believe instruction is even more important in this sport than in some others, because you must consider the "other half" of the team: your horse.

Riding is different than picking up a club and beating a ball until it goes into a hole. As the rider, you *choose* to ride. You make a conscious choice to saddle up and get on. You want to do it. The horse is not given the same choice.

Your Number One Teammate: The Horse

Olympic two-time gold-medalist Joe Fargis once said, "It's not very often that you put a horse in a field with a bunch of jumps and he'll jump around in a beautiful pattern."

Horses have no understanding of why they trot around in endless circles, start and stop at a particular place, or jump fence after fence. Jumping is not something that interests them. They would prefer to eat and sleep and run around on their own time. Many horses are quite talented jumpers and do a very good job, but the work is never a deliberate choice they make.

We teach horses to jump. We are the reason they do it. Therefore, we have a huge responsibility to do our part as best we can, so that the horse's end of the deal is as comfortable as possible.

3.1 *When we ride, we take the horses out of their natural, normal environment and ask them to do things that they have no reason to do.*

Good Horses Make Good Riders

Experience is the best teacher. The more different horses you can ride, the more experiences you will have and the more quickly you will learn things.

If, however, you must choose between riding one good horse and riding several bad horses, you are better off riding the one good horse. Good horses make good riders. A good horse is the best riding instructor you will ever have. The more positive experiences you can have on good horses, the better habits you will be able to build.

Your Coach: The Instructor

Because every team has two pieces—horse and rider—it is critical that you have someone knowledgeable to help you. A riding instructor can help improve your form, which will lead to better function. He will help you understand theory. He will help you learn how to determine goals and work toward them. And, perhaps most importantly, he will help you understand how to put all the little pieces of riding together into some unified, effective whole.

A riding instructor controls safety. He gives you exercises, provides experiences to help you learn, and offers feedback. He can demonstrate the skills he teaches. He can help your horse learn something so that your horse, in turn, can help *you* learn something.

Your instructor is also a manager. He manages your time, your horse's soundness, and your career so both you and your horse are still enjoying the sport several years later.

Furthermore, if he is any good at all, your instructor helps you learn life lessons and skills that you can rely on, both on the horse and off.

3.2 *Riders of all ages and all levels need instruction throughout their careers. You are never too good to learn from someone else. Here, I'm getting pointers from Archie Cox, a top young West Coast trainer with a fresh perspective.*

Staying in the Game

Your need for instruction declines proportionately as you gain expertise. In other words, if you are a rank beginner, you need 100 percent supervision. Not only is this critical from a safety perspective, but it is also the key to building good habits and developing correct position from the very beginning.

If you are an expert, you owe it to yourself to find ways to continue learning. Your skills will improve from reading books, taking lessons, talking to your peers, conducting or participating in clinics, or judging horse shows. Though instruction may take a lesser proportion of your riding time as your expertise improves, when it comes to horses, no one will ever know it all.

Choosing an Instructor

Since an instructor is so important, spend some time shopping for a good one.

Go to horse shows. When you see horses and riders that look like they are performing well, find out who teaches them. (Realize, however, that to a certain point, results can be deceiving.) Often, a long-term instructor/student relationship is based on factors other than simply winning classes.

Consider a potential instructor's reputation. If he has written articles or books, read them. See if you agree with his methods.

Talk to people and ask for recommendations. Interview instructors. Let them tell you their mission. Let them tell you their philosophy. You should be comfortable with the person who directs your riding.

For many people, money is a major consideration. Don't be afraid to ask what an instructor's rates are. Watch as many of a potential instructor's students as possible to see how those rates translate into learning time.

Get as much information as possible about an instructor you are considering before you make the move. Take a lesson from each potential instructor before committing yourself to any one person. Doing your homework ahead of time will make it easier for you to put your riding career in your instructor's care.

It is important to ride with someone whose methods you believe in and who you trust. This is much more than a "success" issue. It is a safety issue. You shouldn't necessarily choose the trainer whose students seem to win the most, but rather the trainer you think can help you the most.

Find someone with whom you can communicate, and who makes you feel confident and totally comfortable. As you start to perfect your riding and begin working toward your goals, you shouldn't need to worry about your relationship with your trainer. You need to be able to focus completely on your riding needs.

Instructors versus Clinicians

Both regular instruction and clinic attendance can benefit your riding education. Neither is more important than the other. You must determine which is most effective for you.

Riding instructors differ from clinicians in several significant ways. In order to get the most out of the time you spend with each, it helps to understand the basic differences between the two.

15 QUESTIONS TO ASK YOURSELF
BEFORE DECIDING ON AN INSTRUCTOR

1   Do I need instruction? (Yes.)

2   What is important to me?

3   Do I want to show? Do I want to event? Do I want to compete at all?

4   Am I a nervous rider, a competent rider, or a confident one? Do I want to put myself on the line, or have a little less pressure on me?

5   How much traveling do I want to do? Do I want to travel to shows? How far am I willing to travel for lessons?

6   Does it matter whether my instructor is male or female?

7   Does it matter whether my instructor rides?

8   Do I want my instructor to be a competitive show rider or a non-show rider?

9   What experience and background do I want my riding instructor to have?

10   How important is the care and maintenance of the horses to my instructor?

11   How important is a beautiful, state-of-the-art facility?

12   Can I communicate with this person?

13   Do I have confidence in this person? Do I trust his judgment?

14   Does this person have the knowledge that I need?

15   Am I going to be satisfied with this person?

The Instructor: With You for the Long Haul

To begin with, your riding instructor is someone you are totally comfortable with. You must have complete faith in your instructor and his program, because a riding instructor is with you for the long term.

The instructor/student relationship has a dictatorial aspect to it (for more information, see p. 236). The instructor has the final say in all aspects of the student's career (fig. 3.3).

Because of the nature of the sport—because of the safety issues involved, as well as the very real dangers associated with any kind of riding—the instructor has to be completely in charge. Period. The instructor makes all major (and most minor) decisions until very late in a rider's career.

The Clinician: Short and Sweet

Your relationship with a clinician is considerably different. Regardless of how well you connect with someone personally or professionally, if he is successful in the business, you can take a clinic or two and learn from him.

3.3 The instructor dictates everything from which exercises to practice, to which horse to ride, to which shows you will attend.

You might hate the clinician's methods or philosophy. You can hate 99 percent of what you did at the clinic. But you can still get *something* out of it.

A clinic is a one-time thing. You go, you learn, and it's over. If you don't like it, don't do it again. Clinics are for a quick infusion of information gathering, interest sparking, and knowledge acquisition.

At a clinic, whether you get along with the clinician and whether you have a lot of confidence in him becomes less important. Clinics are a way to open yourself to some new ideas and, hopefully, get the creative-learning juices flowing.

Both regular instruction and attending the occasional clinic are important in a rider's education. They go together. Attending a clinic will probably give you some new information. Then, if you have a riding instructor that you are comfortable and confident with, you can talk to him about the information

10 QUESTIONS TO ASK
A POTENTIAL RIDING INSTRUCTOR

1 What is your main objective with your students?

2 What successes have you had?

3 How long has your average student been with you? Do your students continue to ride as they become adults?

4 What other horse sports or riding disciplines do your students participate in?

5 What different experiences have you had as an instructor? As a rider?

6 What is your showing experience?

7 Who were your instructors?

8 What books do you recommend?

9 What horse shows do you like and why?

10 What do you think is important/unimportant about riding, equitation, and competition?

you have gleaned. A competent instructor will not react out of fear, jealousy, or emotion, but will give an honest response to your questions and your thoughts on the clinic.

Private Lessons versus Group Instruction

Lessons can be private, one-on-one learning situations or interactive group classes. What is best for the rider generally depends on the level of riding experience.

Riding Alone

When you start riding—when you are actually *learning how to ride*—I believe it is critical that you begin with private lessons.

I always start beginning riders on the lead line, with the student on one horse and myself on another horse. The student's horse is attached to a lead line that I hold throughout the lesson.

Ponying a beginner on another horse is becoming a lost art, but I feel it is the best way to start a rider. The student can ride on the trail right away. The instructor can be right next to the student and hold onto him if necessary. Ponying the beginner puts the instructor in a situation where he can control and manage the whole learning process.

Once you know the basics of riding, however, private lessons are often a disadvantage. One of the main reasons for this is because you lose the ability to learn from others.

Still, sometimes even advanced riders need private lessons. Occasionally, people can get so emotional that they don't work as well in a group as they do by themselves. If you are scared, or if something is seriously troubling you or the horse, it may help to have some private time with your instructor to work through the problem.

Similarly, if you are getting ready for a special event and there is a particular piece of the ride that is bothering you, a private lesson or two might be necessary.

Riding in Groups

The biggest advantage in taking group lessons is the ability to learn by example. You watch other students doing exactly the same exercise on the same day as you. You learn from their horses, their perspectives, and their different backgrounds. After watching others, you can try the exercise. You can quickly get a feel for what you do understand and identify what you don't understand.

Riding in a group gives you a huge increase in exposure to a single lesson. You have several opportunities to try a given exercise. You can also watch each of the other riders try the same exercise several times. Most beneficial of all, your horse gets a break while you continue learning.

In a group situation, you have a mini audience of your peers and your competition (fig. 3.4). Competition in lessons can become fierce. In other words, if two students are struggling with the same exercise, there is a certain amount of natural competitiveness that will encourage both riders to improve more quickly.

Another benefit of group lessons is that they require you to perform an exercise at a particular moment. The moment arrives, you know what you have to do, you have to do it *now*, and you have to do it in front of people. Learning to perform on command is a great skill booster.

3.4 *Every time you are in a group, you have a chance to practice riding in front of an audience, as you would at a horse show.*

The Student's Perspective

Safety is the number one reason for getting qualified riding instruction. You have to learn how to ride, how to be around horses, and how to compete successfully and safely. Rarely can that happen to any significant degree if you only work by yourself in your backyard.

As a student, I want to learn the skills that will make me a more effective rider. I don't want to spend time with a teacher who just tells me what to do every step of the way. Instead, I want a teacher who instills confidence and security.

The Disciplined Rider

Discipline gets you what you want. Everybody wants success. Discipline makes that possible. The more disciplined you are, the more progress you will make.

In other words, if you have an opportunity to work with somebody, you need to be disciplined enough to be sure that you, above all else, show up on time (preferably early). Arrive organized, ready to go, well turned-out, and interested enough to pay 100 percent attention to whoever is trying to help you.

A lot of people think they would like to ride without much discipline, but they are the ones who, in the end, won't do what it takes to be successful. They don't have the drive to stick with their riding and meet their goals. Then, they are disappointed and move on.

If you don't discipline yourself, you won't make steady improvement. You will get sloppy and lazy. Then you will probably quit riding, or change instructors, because you haven't met with success. The whole time, however, your lack of discipline works against you.

Building and Strengthening the Student/Instructor Relationship

Your instructor is not responsible for instilling you with the drive to ride well. He shouldn't have to tell you, "Try harder. Work harder. Practice more. Get the job done. Push yourself a little bit more."

That is tiring. And, it is not his job.

The students I really enjoy teaching are the ones who push themselves and try hard. I want to be the one saying, "Settle down. You are doing fine. You are working too hard. Easy does it."

My favorite student never talks during a lesson, unless it is to ask an intelligent, pertinent question. He tries too hard. He is always early. He never complains about his bills or his duties. He is the kind of person I will stand on my head to help.

I want to help the student who is helping himself. I *don't* want to help the student who just sits in the ring waiting for me, and who gives the entire responsibility of his ride over to me.

Your instructor wants to help you learn. He wants to help you teach yourself how to ride. He wants to give you information and help you understand it. The best way to get the most from your lessons is to keep the door of communication wide open.

Pass It On

As a student, I want somebody to teach me in such a way that I learn the information and assimilate it. After the instruction is over, I want to be able to continue to teach myself.

Most students will say they want to study with instructors who will help them win and bring them success—but I go one more than that. I want to be taught things that I can use to progress on my own.

As your skills and knowledge increase, you shouldn't always need someone to help you choose the right bit or to tell you when to pull on the reins. Your trainer should teach you how to make a horse light, how to gauge distances, or how to engage the hindquarters. Then, when you can understand the theory and the process, you can use that knowledge again down the road on another horse, or in another situation.

A good teacher will teach his students how to teach. Sometimes that means teaching themselves; sometimes it means teaching others.

Teaching helps you to understand a particular exercise: both in theory and in execution. In many respects you haven't really learned something until you can talk about it and teach it to somebody else.

Venturing Out on Your Own

Many instructors—myself included—have a tendency to be "control freaks." As I explained earlier, at the beginning of your riding career, this is a necessity. The instructor must be in complete control and demand your absolute compliance to everything he says. Your life literally depends on it.

At some point, however, you must learn to think for yourself—to take responsibility for your actions. If you don't, you run the risk of becoming too reliant on your instructor to make any significant progress.

Every instructor must realize that as students improve, they should be allowed to do more on their own. When you have gained a foundation that will allow you to have some success making your own choices, your instructor should recognize your abilities and encourage them.

Becoming a thinking rider doesn't just happen. It has to be planned. As a teacher, I am constantly trying to create a rider who doesn't need me. I want to produce a competent trainer who is self-reliant and who doesn't require my input for every phase of the training process.

The way to become a thinking rider is to gradually do more and more on your own. Maybe you will begin by warming the horse up on your own. That might lead to doing a complete schooling session without the instructor's input. As your skills improve, your instructor may ask you to school a green horse or analyze a part of a course by yourself.

Gradually accept responsibility for more and more difficult things. You must start to build experiences handling such things as course analysis, schooling problems, flighty horses, and training concerns on your own, without the instructor there to guide you every step of the way.

If at First You Don't Succeed…

While it is important that you are not completely cut loose all at once, when you *do* try something by yourself, you should be allowed to make your own mistakes. It doesn't do you any good if your instructor tells you to work on your own and then watches you and spits out comments the whole time.

You will inevitably have a few failures. Remember that your mistakes— even the spectacular debacles—are not luxuries. If you learn from them, you will ultimately become a better horseperson.

4

Goal-Oriented Riding

Ride with Purpose

When working on your riding, you owe it to yourself, your horse, and your instructor to do the best job you can. That starts with the basic assumption that your practice will ultimately lead to improvement. In other words, you must believe that you can actually meet (and eventually exceed) your goals.

Though a preoccupation with ribbons is detrimental to your riding—not to mention your enjoyment of the sport—I encourage all my students to set goals for themselves (figs. 4.1 A & B).

Once you know where you would like to end up, then you have to back-track, break that goal into pieces, and develop the skills you will need in order to achieve your end. This process will determine your course of study. It will give you a "map" for systematically learning all the pieces that will enable you to attain your goal.

The trick is to know what you want in the end. But, don't let your ultimate destination blind you to the steps that must be taken along the way.

Don't Ride for Results

When setting goals for your riding, beware of focusing only on results. I have seen many riders concentrate so intensely on their ultimate goals that they completely destroy their chances of achieving them.

4.1 A *Goals challenge you to grow.*

B *They infuse your riding with purpose.*

The best argument I have against concentrating only on results is simple: it doesn't work. With too many riders, a single unforeseen setback can so derail their "Master Plan" they never recover their momentum.

I have an older student, a woman in her sixties, who has ridden with me for over twelve years. She is always saying to me, "I just want to be consistent."

This student is typical of many riders. She is not a bad rider, by any means. But, the more she worries about being consistent, doing well, and winning, the worse she performs.

I tell her over and over again, "If you obsess about consistency, you won't have it. Forget about measuring up to what you have done in the past. Concentrate instead on what you are doing right now. Enjoy it and do it to the best of your ability."

When I can finally get her to relax, forget about her "results" for a little bit, focus only on what she is doing, and enjoy the ride, that is when she masters a new skill or wins her class.

Preoccupation with being successful is no guarantee that success is just around the corner. Often, concentrating on your riding at the moment, instead of worrying about winning or placing, is what brings the best results.

What It Takes

The most important thing for any rider is *interest*. In order to succeed in anything, you have to really want to.

Of course, it doesn't hurt if the rider is tall, thin, and athletic. If you are graced with the ideal body type, count your blessings. As for talent, hand-eye coordination, depth perception and so on—all these are important attributes. But, none of them outweigh interest.

Competitive riding can be very challenging, especially as you move up within the ranks of your discipline or division. To ride well requires a long-term commitment. It is ultimately very satisfying, but you have to be interested in making the most of your abilities.

In any case, realistic expectations are essential. In the case of my older student, her dream of consistency was as unrealistic as riding in the Olympic games. I had to tell her that she was being completely unreasonable. She will never be consistently in the ribbons. She will never be a great rider. And that's fine.

After thinking about her situation overnight, my student came back to me and said that for her, studying equitation was like going to college and never being smart enough to pass, but enjoying the parties anyway.

This student knows that if she studies very hard, once in a while, everything will come together. When that happens at a show, she will ride well, she will receive high scores, and do well in the placings. If it happens at home, she will still have great personal satisfaction and a sense of accomplishment.

I believe every rider needs a certain amount of competitiveness to survive. A good rider will want to be able to push and give everything he has when it counts. But, you only set yourself up for failure if you ask yourself to do something that is completely beyond your ability. Realize that everybody has limitations. Just relax and enjoy the parties along the way.

4.2 *Riding at the front of the field is a coveted position—an "Ultimate Goal"—in foxhunting. If you hone your skills and keep an eye on your goals, you will someday be in a position to realize them.*

Planning for Your Future

There is tremendous benefit in setting long-term riding goals (fig. 4.2). Planning for the future can help you more readily identify what you need to work on *right now*.

Goal planning always follows a predictable path:

1 Start at the end: identify your "Ultimate Goal."
2 Set a feasible date for achieving that goal.
3 Identify key things that will help you achieve your goal. Write them down in order of which must happen first.
4 Periodically reevaluate and reassess your goals.

Riding toward the Ultimate Goal

Let's say your Ultimate Goal is to be the World Champion Hunter Rider/ Amateur Owner Rider of the Year. Determining a reasonable date for achieving your goal will depend on your current abilities.

Your pathway toward reaching that goal would include learning to ride hunters at home, beginning to compete as an Adult Amateur hunter rider, becoming successful as an Adult Amateur, beginning to compete in the Amateur Owner Hunter division, and becoming increasingly successful within this division.

If your Ultimate Goal is to be able to foxhunt competently and safely in time for a particular season, you would start out riding in the ring in lessons. Then, you would ride cross-country in lessons, and then you might do a little hound-jogging or ride cross-country more extensively and over rougher terrain. Next, you would learn to cub hunt. Finally, your hard work would culminate in having the horses, the confidence, and the ability to ride on an easy hunt. More difficult hunts would follow.

If you approach your Ultimate Goal from the bottom, looking up, it is too easy to become overwhelmed or bogged down in the details. Coming at your goal from the end—knowing what you want to achieve—will allow you to identify the various mini-goals along the way.

Step 1: *Start at the End*

So go ahead: ask yourself, "What is my long-term goal?"

Let's say that your answer is "riding in the Olympics." Though becoming an Olympian may not be terribly realistic, there is nothing wrong with having big dreams, provided you have the talent, the resources, and the time frame to allow you to achieve them.

Step 2: *Set a Date for Success*

Once you have identified an attainable Ultimate Goal, determine a reasonable time frame to allow yourself to achieve it.

If you are twelve now and just learning to ride, you may be ready to try out for the Olympic team, if you are lucky, when you are forty-two. That leaves thirty years of training ahead of you. (If you are currently in your forties and just learning to ride, you must come to terms with reality. In all likelihood, riding in the Olympics is not in your future. If you don't have the necessary

4.3 Before you can achieve your goal, you must know what it is. It is critical for both you and your instructor to understand your goal. Here, both the student and I are aware of her end goal, and we're discussing specifics for one round along the way.

resources, don't stubbornly cling to unrealistic goals and take the joy out of learning.)

Step 3: What Has to Happen First

The next question you must ask yourself is, "What will I need to know in order to make my goal possible?"

For our example, let's say that you think doing well in the Hunt Seat Equitation Finals is an important step in your Olympic quest. Therefore, winning a ribbon in the finals now becomes your temporary Ultimate Goal. Dreams of the Olympics are fine, but your immediate *work* will be toward the finals.

This means that your entire focus will be on equitation for the time being. When you are done—when you are successful in the Hunt Seat Equitation division—then perhaps you will move on to riding jumpers as you identify the next step toward the Olympics.

Set actual, mini-achievable goals. These might include:

* Qualify for the finals this year.
* Make it into the second round next year.
* Win a ribbon, or win the finals, the following year.

As with everything in life, finances must be a consideration in your goal planning. If you can only afford one horse, you will have to make a conscious decision to do the Hunt Seat Equitation divisions first. Then, plan to sell that horse and get one better suited to the Jumper division when you are ready to advance.

Your goals need not be so lofty as being a rider on the Olympic team or a World Champion, but aiming high can be inspiring. Try to be realistic in your dreams so you don't set yourself up for failure, and try to understand what shortcomings you might have, and take them into consideration.

There are any number of things that can keep you from your goals. But nothing will ever happen for you until you set a plan for yourself. Decide what you want to do. Then plan a series of steps to bring you closer to the end you envision.

Step 4: Evaluate Your Progress

Nothing high-tech can beat a list made with a paper and pencil. Write your goals down and hold yourself accountable for them. Check them at the end of

Goal-Oriented Riding ~ 43

every year. Then write down what you will work on the *next* year to bring you closer to your destination.

Remember: there is no shame in failure. But, if you do not try, you will never succeed.

Goal Setting: Low and Slow

I always tell my students, half joking and half serious, that the key to success is low expectations.

Whenever you are setting goals, set what comes to mind. Then cut it in half. The worst that could happen would be reaching that goal too soon, or too easily. The only danger in that is possibly feeling too good about yourself. You will become confident, which will allow you to raise your goals and start again.

Low Expectations

Start with knowing what you want. Once you have an idea of where you would like to go with your riding, break your goals into small, identifiable pieces and allot plenty of time to reach them.

If you think it will take a month to get something done, give yourself two months.

If you think that you want to do ten perfect jumps, try to get five.

Don't overtax yourself or your horse. Take extra time. Don't rush through things. Before you know it, you will reach your goals faster than if you tried too hard and did too much.

Winning Isn't Everything

Your goals don't need to be "wins." Depending on your level of ability, some examples of worthwhile goals might be:

- Comfortably jumping a cross-rail
- Consistently getting the lead you want at the canter
- Completing a 3' course
- Riding well without stirrups
- Developing independent hands
- Moving up into a new competitive division

- Placing in the national finals
- Training a green horse

Try to set realistic goals, and allow yourself a reasonable amount of time to attain those goals. When you reach a goal you have set, raise your sights. After every success, increase your expectations and set a new goal to work toward.

The Quest for Perfection

Many riders make the mistake of focusing on the outcome of a particular round. They worry about what happens in the show ring more than they care about what happens at any other time. They are so concerned about a potentially poor ride they become a ball of nerves in a constant state of anxiety. Neither they nor their horses can enjoy themselves while competing.

I want my students to be able to perform well when it matters most. But, a great round does not come from obsessing about it beforehand. Instead, it comes from the confidence of solid preparation.

Practice Pieces

Before show season starts, decide what type of course you want to do by season's end. Analyze what kinds of questions are going to be asked of you and your horse as the year progresses. Identify what sorts of reactions and skills you will need in order to do well. Then, break that "end-of-season" course into pieces, and get to work on them.

For example, in a typical hunter course, you need to be able to jump straight lines, forward lines, and slow lines. You need to jump at least one fence off a turn. You need to be able to navigate diagonal lines. You may need to be able to do broken lines or in-and-outs. For handy hunter classes, you may be asked to trot a jump or make tight turns.

You do not do yourself any favors if you start the season without ever determining what sorts of challenges you can expect to see in the ring.

Once you know what the pieces are, you can set about learning the skills and devising exercises to help you master them. Don't practice courses over and over again. Instead, practice skills that will help you put the perfect round together when you need to.

Use a single part of a course as an individual exercise and practice learning to do that part well. (See chapter 11, *Course Work*, to discover how to break a course down into its various parts. You will also find specific exercises to improve your understanding of those parts.)

Practice at home until you have mastered the skills you need. Then, when you are at the show and you see a particular type of line or fence, you and your horse will be able to excel, and all your hard work will pay off.

Beware! Don't Over-Prepare

As you practice and work toward your goals, bear in mind the dangers of over-preparation. This is where learning to manage your time comes into play.

I always tell my students, "You only get so many 'breakthrough' rounds, where everything is exactly right. You will only have four or five best rounds, when everything falls perfectly into place, in a career."

Being over-prepared is when you have practiced too much and your riding becomes rote. It lacks spark and energy. It lacks brilliance.

It is very easy to over-prepare. In today's show ring, over-preparation is a huge problem. It is not at all uncommon to see horses knocking down jumps because they are bored or sore.

An over-prepared horse and rider team delivers a lackluster, unimpressive performance. They are robotic in their movements. They have hit their peak too early—at home in the practice ring, when it didn't count.

Peak Planning

Plan your training so you and your horse peak at the horse show and not at home the week beforehand. A part of the art of competing and the art of training is to get that breakthrough round at a moment when it really matters. Careful preparation is the key to ensuring that you and your horse are in top form when it counts.

4.4 *The ability to deliver your best performance on a particular day is a direct result of your goal planning.*

4.5 *Lessons are about learning, not about achieving perfection.*

When planning a peak performance, as with everything else related to your goals, you must start at the end. Articulate what you want to accomplish during the upcoming season. Have a sense of what you and your horse must be able to do in order to reach your ultimate goal. Identify the different stages of training necessary to get to that goal and work on them.

Your ultimate goal is to ride perfectly when you need it most. That is *not* during a lesson. Lessons are about figuring out pieces of a puzzle, filling your bag of tricks, and developing skills and tools.

Horse shows allow you to put the pieces, tricks, skills, and tools together. To that end, if you think that you need ten horse shows in order to do things right at the "Really Big Event," you must take each of those ten shows into account.

Plan your year all the way to the end. If it is January now, and you want your best performance to happen at a big show on October 15, you must address the following questions:

- Am I entered in the right shows to make qualifying for the October event possible?
- How can I, between now and then, participate in enough horse shows to qualify, but not so many that my horse ends up tired, sour, or lame?
- How can I compete in enough shows so that I am experienced, but still have enough time at home to work on my basics and make sure that I have honed my skills?
- How do I arrive on October 15 having shown in enough pressure situations to be able to be competitive, but without overdoing things and being worn out?
- How much time do I need to rest before the big event in order to be sure that my horse and I are fresh?

There are no easy answers to these questions. But, you do your horse and yourself a huge favor if you address them early in the season, instead of careening toward a major event with no forethought. Ask yourself the pertinent questions. Then, based on your answers, arrive at a plan.

More importantly—as the show season progresses, *follow* your plan. If you find that your plan was too ambitious, by all means reevaluate. But, don't allow early successes to make you overreach your original intentions. That is how horses get injured or sour, and how riders get burnt out.

The Merits of Competition

The notion of a particular round counting more than another concerns some riders. "Why emphasize competition?" they wonder. "How will competing make me a better rider?"

Of course, competition is not necessary. One of its great merits, however, is that it gives you a fairly accurate way to gauge your own progress.

4.6 *Competition allows you to see how you measure up against other riders, and against your own past performances.*

I teach many students who never show. They just enjoy lessons and the process of learning. That is fine, but competing can help perfect skills that won't bloom in a tamer environment.

Competition puts you in a situation that you did not create yourself. Other course designers are never going to build a course exactly as you would. They are not going to hold a horse show in exactly the same place you would normally ride. The ring won't be exactly the same size as you are used to. When you are at home, doing your exercises and riding your courses, you will inevitably tend toward a particular, consistent pattern or program. Competition bumps you out of your comfort bubble.

If you only ride on your own, it is very easy to develop a slanted viewpoint. But, just attending an event—going somewhere else, doing things in a different way, jumping somebody else's courses, competing against other people, and showing in front of different judges—introduces countless variables that will only help develop you as a rider.

Take Note

Throughout the year, I make notes of riding skills that my students still need to work on. I actually write down a list of things that I feel need to be included in our preparation before we head to a big show.

One student's list might include the following:

- Needs to jump more without stirrups
- Uncomfortable with long approaches
- Hands too high / shoulders too round
- Has difficulty keeping the horse's shoulders balanced through turns
- Has problems picking up correct leads

I will only write down things that should already be mastered, or that I know will be tested that year. For instance, if the student is having problems picking up his correct leads, it would be pointless for me to add "flying changes" to the list.

Committing your concerns to paper can help keep yourself on track. It can provide a valuable reference during your practices.

Don't put everything you ever want to be able to do on a horse on one list. Remember: practice riding in manageable pieces.

Gauging Your Progress

Perfection is not a realistic goal for any rider. The point of equitation is to constantly hone your skills and improve your riding.

If over a period of time—one year, five years, or ten years—you steadily move up in the divisions and improve, then you are doing a good job. If you don't seem to be progressing, then perhaps you need to talk to some other trainers or change your program a little bit to make a difference.

Goals are very personal things. Every now and again reflect on your progress and review your program. Decide what you like and don't like about your current approach. Decide how you are going to address what needs to be changed. Then, move on from there.

The Annual Extra

Every year, in addition to the obvious facets of good riding—"heels down," "straight line to the mouth," "ride forward"—I choose one new habit that I want to have adopted by the end of the season.

For instance, one year my "Annual Extra" was to always be sure schooling jumps at horse shows were placed where the footing was good. If they were not, I would deliberately move the jumps to better ground. It became a firm habit, developed over the course of a year, and it is now ingrained in my students, my grooms, and anyone that helps us. When we go to school a horse, we put the jump in good footing.

For the Annual Extra, as with so many other aspects of riding, checklists are invaluable. They allow you to analyze what you want to do and what you actually do. Then you can change what is necessary in order to improve.

Train over Time

Everything in my teaching is designed for the long term. I am not remotely interested in so-called "quick fixes" because in my experience they don't exist. Instead, I am focused on doing what will be right for a horse or a rider in the long run.

The most competent instructor cannot take a talented rider and make him into an equitation medalist or champion jumper competitor overnight. It is important that you understand this from the onset of your riding education.

If You Are Just Beginning

Several years ago, an adult student came to me as a rank beginner. She had only been to one horse show in her life. We set her a goal of becoming a competitive rider in the Amateur Owner Hunter division. Then we broke that goal into pieces.

First, we used a "made" (well-trained) horse and she competed in the Adult Amateur Hunters. Her horse was more of a teacher than a winner, but he gave her some success and allowed her to build her skills and her confidence.

When she was ready to advance, because of monetary restraints, we found a younger horse and worked until she was successful in the Adult Amateur Hunter division.

She sold the young horse for enough money to buy a "more made" horse that was very successful in the 3' Adult Amateur Hunter classes. This horse became her teacher in the 3' 6" Amateur classes. Riding him enabled her to break into the Amateur Owner division. She was able to be competitive and win at the smaller shows. She was also able to take him to some of the larger shows and experience the difference in the level of competition.

When she was ready to move up again, she bought a younger horse that we felt had the potential to be competitive in the Amateur Owner Hunter divisions.

So far, the pursuit of this rider's Ultimate Goal has taken us seven years. She is still at least two years away from reaching that goal. She may make it; she may not. But, taking nine or ten years to go from an absolute beginner to being competitive at rated shows in the 3' 6" division is not at all unusual.

I offer the same advice to all novice riders:

- Start at the beginning.
- Don't rush. Take enough time to do each new thing as well as possible.
- Quality counts. Get the best instructor you can find, the best horse you can ride, and the best tack you can afford. The "best" isn't always the most expensive, but it is rarely the cheapest. In my experience, it is better to have a few, good, top quality items than an assortment of poorly made, low-grade equipment. Get in the habit early of recognizing the value of high quality.
- Every great rider had to begin at some point. Learn all you can and don't get discouraged.

Advice for the Advanced Rider

My advice to riders who are ready to move up to higher levels of competition is much the same as for the beginning rider:

- Spend the time that is necessary to ride well. If you think you can learn to do something in six months, give yourself a year to perfect it.
- Do your best.
- Don't sacrifice quality.
- Get the best help possible.
- Ride the best horses you can find.

  In addition,

- Plan your time and use it effectively.
- Don't let stress interfere with your riding. Keep your anxiety levels to a minimum. If necessary, tone your schooling down.

Above All, Don't Rush!

If you try to get too much done in too short a time, you will end up disinterested, confused, frustrated, sore, or tired—and that won't get you anywhere. Rushing only results in a rider who makes less progress than he would have if he had taken his time and enjoyed the process.

4.7 Don't rush. Riding is more about the journey than the destination. Although this rider is at the beginning of her career, she is clearly enjoying working to build the skills she needs for the future.

You are always better off leaving something on the plate that still needs to be done. Don't try to do everything perfectly all at once. Remember the merits of mastering your riding in bite-sized pieces. That's what keeps trainers, horses, and students fresh.

Riding in Competition

5.1 *Deciding which shows to compete in is a big part of your overall career strategy.*

Choosing a Show

The trick to successful showing, as with everything else, is balance.

A significant part of your schedule should include smaller, simpler shows. These make it easy for you to get results. Those results can include specifics such as winning a certain number of classes or qualifying for a division championship. Results can also be more intangible and involve things like feeling good about your riding or developing confidence over fences.

The easier horse shows give you the opportunity to shine. There, you can compete against other riders who may not yet be up to your level. You can enter the ring knowing that if you do your best, you can end up the winner.

Sometimes, however, to get the most out of a show experience, you need to concentrate less on winning and focus more on stretching yourself.

In addition to the easier shows, your schedule should also include events where the competition is of a significantly higher caliber.

The tougher shows help to balance the easier ones. They expose you to better training, better horses, and better riding. These events also give you the opportunity to experience stricter, more nuanced judging, and more challenging courses. You have the chance to compete in a larger talent pool and see how you measure up.

As you plan out your show season, remember to keep it balanced. If you only attend the easier shows, you will soon have an unrealistically inflated opinion of your abilities. If you only compete in the big, rated shows, chances are you will become discouraged.

Showing involves a big commitment on your part. It takes time, energy, and money. It puts a certain amount of stress on you and your horse. For these reasons, make your show selections wisely. To maximize your show experience, strike a balance between events where you are competitive and events where you may not be in the ribbons as often, but you can learn from watching others.

Understanding the Sport

Many divisions exist within the world of hunt seat riding. Though every circuit and every show has its own specific requirements for a class, certain principles remain constant.

The judge focuses on different areas, depending on whether you are showing in equitation, hunter, or jumper classes. In order to compete effectively, it helps to know what aspects of your performance will be evaluated.

Hunt Seat Equitation: Perfect Position

In Hunt Seat Equitation, the performance of the rider is all that matters (fig. 5.2). Classes are judged subjectively, with an emphasis on the rider's position, poise, balance, and horsemanship. If the horse performs poorly, however, it reflects on the rider's ability, and must be taken into consideration.

Equitation classes never award prize monies to the winners. The amateur rider is considered the winner of the class, and the ribbon, trophy, or medal he receives is his reward for a job well done.

5.2 *The purpose of the Hunt Seat Equitation division is to develop riders who focus on style and correctness. It was created to make riders aware of good position and to create a solid foundation built on strong basic skills.*

JUDGE'S CARD
TESTING THE EQUITATION RIDER

Everything about the equitation class focuses on the rider. The horse's conformation, movement, and general abilities are not taken into consideration, except for how they reflect the rider's ability. Even the horse's jumping faults are not penalized, unless they result from the rider's influence.

The equitation rider may be asked to perform one or more of the nineteen approved United States Equestrian Federation (USEF) tests during a class. The test requirements are easily accessible. If you intend to show in equitation classes, it is important that you know them, become familiar with them, and incorporate the tests in your home training. (For more information regarding the USEF tests, see the *Appendix*, p. 253.)

Equitation faults are discussed in detail in chapter 9, *Perfect Position*. Certain faults, however, will result in mandatory disqualification from the class. These include:

- Not having the horse under control at all times
- Tying or affixing the rider's leg to the stirrup or stirrup leather in any way, anywhere on the competition grounds
- Inappropriate show ring attire
- Three refusals
- Fall of horse or rider
- Riding off course

For the most part, the division is open only to junior riders. It is intended to educate the rider, to hone his skills, and develop the tools he will need for a lifetime with horses.

Hunters: Style and Elegance

The perfect hunter is beautiful in every way. He is spotless, graceful, athletic, and well-mannered. He moves effortlessly across the ground.

Hunters are judged according to their style, their correctness of gait and

5.3 *In the hunter world, the horse is the center of attention.*

movement, their overall attitude, and the quality of their performance (fig. 5.3). The most important criterion is the horse's style over fences. His body should remain straight, without twisting in the air. The front legs should be folded neatly, with knees even and lifted high.

When he jumps, the hunter's head and neck stretch out and down. His entire topline rounds in an arc.

Quality is the hunter's hallmark. Because long days in the hunt field require a sizeable energy reserve, the ideal hunter moves fluidly and effortlessly with minimal knee action. A top hunter is relaxed and clearly enjoys his job. He appears eminently easy to ride.

As the rider, you are not technically judged in the hunter ring. It is your responsibility, however, to present the horse in his best light.

The more relaxed you are, the better your horse will appear to the judge. Your goal is to demonstrate how easy and enjoyable your mount is to ride.

Hunter over Fences

Judging begins the moment the horse and rider enter the ring and lasts until they leave.

Throughout the course, the judges look for consistency, confidence, grace, and good style. A steady pace, brilliant form, and can-do attitude are rewarded. The horse is expected to stay straight in the middle of each jump and easily maneuver through the corners. Knocked-down rails and refusals are penalized.

JUDGE'S CARD
EVALUATING THE HUNTER HORSE

As a hunter judge, I look for a horse that is beautiful and consistent. I want to see a horse that I would happily ride for miles on a foxhunt.

The most beautiful horse with the best conformation and the easiest gaits will get the highest marks. The hunter with the smoothest round and the best jumping efforts will win the class.

COMMON FAULTS

- Pace changes or unevenness
- Rubbing or touching the jumps
- Uneven front legs while jumping
- Twisting the body over the fence
- Jumping a fence off-center
- Unhappy expression (ears back, twitching tail)
- Open mouth
- High head on the flat or over a fence
- Refusing a fence

- Knocking a rail down
- Cross-cantering
- Cantering on the wrong lead
- Hanging a leg
- Knees pointing down
- Running away
- Bucking or kicking out

DISQUALIFICATIONS

- Lameness
- Three refusals

Hunter under Saddle

In flat classes, the judges evaluate the horse's manners and movement at the walk, trot, and canter.

The horse should work quietly in a group, with only light contact on his mouth at all gaits. He should appear relaxed and happy. A competitive hunter has his ears up, his neck stretched out, and his head down. He is alert and exudes calm, capable confidence.

Jumpers: Speed and Accuracy

Jumping is a performance sport with quantifiable points and rules. In the jumper divisions, judging is entirely objective. A jumper's placing in a given event is based on faults accrued for various errors including refusals, run-outs, rails down, falls, and going over the optimum time.

> ## JUDGE'S CARD
> ## JUDGING JUMPERS
>
> Determining a jumper's score for any given round is not difficult. The scoring system is consistent throughout the sport. Refusals, touching or knocking down rails, and taking too long to complete the course will accrue faults. Falls, repeated refusals, or going off course result in elimination from competition.
>
> In addition to faults amassed on the course, the judge may also eliminate a rider in the following circumstances, in or out of the show ring, anywhere on the show grounds:
>
> - The rider is considered inappropriately dressed to appear before the public.
> - Failure to wear a suitable helmet with three-point harness when jumping in any event sanctioned by the Fédération Equestre Internationale (FEI).
> - The rider is excessively aggressive with the use of whips, spurs, or poles.
> - The rider has his stirrups, stirrup leathers, or feet tied or secured in any way.

Jumper classes may be divided with respect to either the horse's or the rider's age and experience. Where jumpers are concerned, style is secondary to speed and agility. The fastest clean round *always* wins, regardless of the horse's form over fences (fig. 5.4).

The Balanced Competitor

Regardless of which branch of competition you pursue, remember the importance of maintaining a balance in your riding. If taken to the extreme, every discipline has the potential for fostering an unhealthy emphasis on a particular aspect.

Equitation riders can focus so much on themselves that they become mechanical "robots," rigidly riding in endless circles and drilling all the energy, brilliance, and joy out of their performance.

5.4 *The fast pace of jumper classes requires boldness, athleticism, and a certain amount of aggressiveness in both horses and riders.*

10 NECESSARY PREPARATIONS FOR A SUCCESSFUL SHOW

So much of having a successful show experience is related to logistics. As much as possible, be prepared days before the event. Know where the event is being held and have reliable directions to get you there.

A great recipe for disaster includes:

- Arriving late because you had to stop for gas
- Wrinkled and dirty show clothes
- Muddy or dusty show boots
- Not knowing which class you are in
- Incorrectly filled-out entries
- Leaving your checkbook at home

I have spent the better part of my life getting ready for shows, going to shows, returning home from shows, and regrouping after shows. Regardless of how big or small—how important or trivial—a particular event may be in my overall goal planning, certain preparations are essential every time.

Taking care of the following things can help set you up for success:

5.5 *Bathe, clip, and trim the horse ahead of time so he is ready when you get to the show.*

1 Know what you can do. Before you head off to a show, practice what you think might happen—plus a little bit extra. If you have to jump 3' 6" for your division at the show, be comfortable jumping 3' 9" fences at home. Don't overdo it. Don't drill and drill and drill. But, know that you are more than capable of doing what your classes will require of you.

2 Have your paperwork in order. Get your entries in on time. Have copies of your horse's registration and proof of your memberships and affiliations. Make sure your horse has a current Coggins test and all of his necessary inoculations, and have the papers to prove it. Have a copy

of the show schedule readily available. Know which classes you will be showing in, in which rings, on which days.

3 Get your horse ready. Have him sound, shod, and well-schooled at least a week beforehand. Bathe and clip him before you leave for the show.

4 Plan ahead. Take traffic, weather, and road conditions into consideration. Plan for things that can go wrong such as detours, missed exits, and construction. Allow room for emergencies in your schedule. Give yourself a buffer of time to arrive, unload, and acclimate to the show grounds.

5 Have your truck and trailer ready. Have them licensed, insured, and clean. See that the tires are aired up and in good condition. Make sure the lights and brakes work. The day before you need to leave, have gas in the tank, check fluid levels, hitch up, and be ready to hit the road.

5.6 *Clean your tack until it shines.*

6 Prepare your clothes. Show clothes and boots should be spotless. Take along an extra clean shirt and gloves. Be sure every piece of your outfit is accounted for and is in pristine condition.

7 Clean your tack. This includes washing your saddle pads, leg wraps, and blankets. Everything—halters, bridles, girths, saddles, martingales, bits, and stirrups—should shine.

8 Pack the night before. Don't forget horse feed, buckets, grooming tools, or first aid supplies. Pack your lunch money and your cell phone. Pack comfortable traveling clothes, bottled water, and your toothbrush.

9 Bring extras along. Prepare yourself for equipment failures. Take an extra bridle, bit, and girth, and have additional sets of reins and stirrup leathers available.

10 Arrive on time—clean, rested, and ready to show.

5.7 *No one will ever turn in a perfect round. But someone will win the class.*

Hunter riders can become so myopically obsessed with appearance that they become blind to the merits of less lovely horses. They run the risk of seeing the horse as nothing more than a beautiful, pricey object, rather than a living, contributing part of the team.

Jumper enthusiasts can easily fall into the trap of pushing their horses to jump too high or go too fast in order to capture prize money.

No part of any show is more important than the well-being of you and your horse. Before you go too far down the road of intense competition, commit yourself to putting your needs and the needs of your horse above the temptation for ribbons or glory. Your riding career will span a much greater time frame— and you will be much more satisfied with your accomplishments—if you resolve not to ride at the horse's expense.

Making the Most of Your Classes

Remember that in each class at each show, you are evaluated only against the horses and riders competing against you *at that particular time.*

In the show ring, you are not squaring off against some unattainable ideal. Instead, you are asking for the judge's informed opinion as to how you and your horse compare to the others in your class.

Bear in mind that the results of a class, a show, or an event hold true only for one person (the judge) at that moment in time. Show results are a helpful benchmark in your continuing progress as a rider, but you should never give them more weight or more importance than they deserve.

It may be helpful to think of each class as having an "On" and "Off" switch. As you enter the ring, approach it as if you have a job to do. The switch is "On." The class is the only thing you have to do at that time. Focus on it. Forget about everything else. Do the absolute best you can.

When the class is over, the switch is "Off." For better or worse, you are done with that job. It is over. There is nothing more you can do to improve your performance. Put it behind you and set your sights on your next class.

Keep the End in Sight

As we discussed earlier, in chapter 4 (see "Planning for Your Future," p. 40), success begins at the end. You have to know what you want to do before you can achieve it. This is especially true with regards to showing.

As you plan your show year, identify the key events ahead of time. Keep these events in mind if questions arise about your horse's soundness, his schooling, or your own readiness. For instance, if your horse is becoming sore, you might have to skip a planned schooling show this weekend in order to be ready for a more important event in three weeks.

Map out your schedule with your goals in mind. Adhere to your plan while it is working. But, don't be afraid to change things and reevaluate them if they are not going the way you had hoped.

6

The Winning Edge

Winning Defined

This chapter focuses almost exclusively on *winning*. While the term "winning" generally refers to placing highly in a class or other formal competitive event, it can mean other things as well.

- If your goal is to jump a 3' course, and you work at it—the day you jump the course, you are a winner.
- If you want to compete in a local horse show, expose your horse to new things, and ride in a class or two without losing your cool—the day you survive a show as a sportsmanlike participant (whether or not you bring home a ribbon), you are a winner.
- If having independent hands or keeping your heels down is a weak point in your riding, and you work and work and *work* at it—the day you master the technique, you are a winner. Even if no one else is around to see it, you and your horse will know that you have won.

As a competitor and instructor, I tend to focus on competition. I appreciate the ways that the show ring can benefit and stretch the rider. Many students, however, find that an emphasis on correct riding is challenging and rewarding in and of itself, without necessarily culminating in the show ring.

Your competition can take many forms. It may be the other riders in the show ring. It may be an uncoordinated or unresponsive body part. It may be a block of fear in your mind. Whatever stands between you and your goals is

6.1 *Whether or not you choose to show, all serious riding is a form of competition.*

your competition. This section explores how to face those obstacles and overcome them.

It's All in Your Head

In some respects, thinking is one of the worst things you can do for your riding.

If you are thinking and over-analyzing too much, you are probably not focusing on how things *feel*. All the thought in the world won't help you move in time with the horse's rhythm. On the contrary, it is much more apt to distract you from focusing on how that rhythm feels, how the horse's movement affects your body, and how your movements affect the horse.

Your thoughts can hinder you in other ways, as well. The concept of mental energy, whether it is positive or negative, has great validity. When your thoughts are full of positive energy, they can help you. But, when they contain negative energy, they work against you.

Positive energy, for example, is when you assume you can win the class you are entered in. You don't belabor the issue and make winning the focal point of your existence. A calm confidence, however, allows you to start analyzing what you need to do to win and to act accordingly

Doubts and second-guessing are examples of negative energy. They sap your confidence and can sabotage your best physical efforts.

If you enter a class thinking, "My horse isn't as expensive as the others. Maybe I should have warmed up more. I don't think the judge likes me. I probably shouldn't be here…" it will be next to impossible for you to turn in a winning ride.

If you don't believe in yourself, it plainly shows in your riding—in your posture, your position, and your overall expression. Furthermore, if you are constantly doubting or questioning yourself, then you are not focusing on the job at hand. Failure becomes inevitable.

Confidence: The Self-Fulfilling Prophecy

The single most valuable aspect of a winner's attitude is confidence.

The more I pay attention to competitors at all levels, the more I see that the people who win the most are the people who *assume* they are going to win. That assumption forms a quiet, capable core of their riding.

If you are not a confident rider, your horse will be the first to know. Confidence may be even more important in riding than in other sports, because you instantly transmit your confidence (or lack of it) to the other half of the team—your horse.

A winning attitude assumes that you can win. Assuming you can win (and knowing that you have done your homework) allows you to relax a bit, block out any distractions, and focus only on doing what is necessary for the best possible outcome.

Once you make the assumption that you are going to win, that assumption gives you the confidence that you *will* win. The confidence comes from knowing you have the capability to do whatever you need to do. It allows you to draw on the skills you have practiced, to become a self-fulfilling prophecy, and ride to victory.

6.2 *The expression of both horse and rider exudes the confidence and focus necessary for competition. Confidence is born of practice. It comes from knowing, through experience, exactly what you and your horse are capable of.*

Developing Your Mental "Game"

It is safe to say that when showing, 75 to 90 percent of your performance is mental. In fact, the tougher and more advanced your level of competition, the more mental preparedness plays a part.

Your mental outlook won't give you physical skills that you have not yet developed. But, it will help you make the most of what you have practiced.

In other words, if you ride beautifully at home, but don't at the horse show, you need to improve your mental "game." If, however, you ride badly at home, a positive attitude won't help you in the show ring.

You must first develop a solid base of physical skills. Then, you have to train your mind to manage those skills.

Physical practice is crucial to improving your mental game. You must teach your muscles to respond in a particular way in a given situation. The more you are aware of what you can do, the more you boost your confidence. Confidence in yourself gives you a positive attitude toward trying more things. The more things you successfully accomplish, the more you boost your confidence. It's a self-feeding, circular scenario.

6.3 *A strong mental game plan begins with honestly analyzing and evaluating a situation. It is rooted in knowing what you can and cannot do. This rider is taking a moment to plan her round. She is visualizing perfection before she ever enters the ring.*

Ride with Vision

The exercise of *visualizing* can be very helpful to your riding. When visualizing, you can minutely examine a course or prepare for an event for as long as you wish while saving your horse's legs and energy for when it matters most.

For instance, let's say you have a 3' course coming up in a few hours. Rather than working your horse to calm *your* nerves, put him away and work on visualizing instead.

To get the most from visualizing, it may help to refer to a drawing of the course. Go somewhere quiet, with no distractions and focus on what will be required of you.

Think about your course as completely as possible, in as many ways as possible:

- Imagine what the course will feel like from start to finish. Imagine how you *want* it to feel.
- Imagine how the necessary pace will feel.
- Think about each line of jumps individually. Try to feel how you will ride each line and each jump.
- Think about every turn individually. Try to feel how you will ride each turn.
- Identify the parts of the course that will be easy for you.
- Identify the parts of the course that will be difficult for you. Then see in your "mind's eye" how you will make them work.
- Over and over again, visualize riding the best round possible.

6.4 *Having a clear understanding of the course layout before you get on the horse is a huge part of the rider's job. It can help you visualize the perfect round.*

Visualize great rounds. Imagine perfection. If you visualize a picture-perfect, beautiful round, you have *such* a better chance of getting what you want.

This exercise can give you the feeling of a positive experience before you actually *do* it. Getting the course right in your head can significantly improve your chances of getting it exactly right in reality.

If, on the other hand, all you can think about is chipping, or crashing and burning on the course ("There's no way I'm going to make that oxer!"), more than likely, that is what will happen.

Positive and negative mental energy are as important to your riding when you are sitting in a chair visualizing as when you are on the horse and headed toward a fence. Whenever possible, imagine things going perfectly. Use your mental energy to make your imagination work *for* you rather than against you.

Becoming a Good Competitor

Good competitors—no matter how talented—have to work very hard for their skills. The best competitors are those who are hungry and driven to succeed. A good competitor is also relaxed and able to downplay the stress that inevitably comes with trying to do one's best.

6.5 *A good competitor is confident in the abilities he has spent hours practicing and developing. As we enter the ring at the Lake Placid Horse Show, it is obvious that both horse and rider are well-prepared to compete.*

When working with my students, I talk about these things a lot. I talk about desire, interest, and work. I talk about effort and struggling and fighting and driving yourself to be the best rider possible. I continually suggest to my students that they are capable of good riding.

Some of my students are good riders and some are bad riders. I treat them all the same. I don't coddle them. I don't overprotect them. Babying a rider doesn't do anyone any favors.

All of my students—regardless of age, weight, body build, and ability—work at improving their equitation. They all ride without stirrups. They do their two-point work, their flatwork, and the difficult exercises. I make them struggle and sweat. They do it because they want to improve.

The responsibility, ultimately, is yours. If you want to win, you need to be committed. You have to work hard. You need to be motivated and self-disciplined. No one, including your instructor, can make you a winner. The drive and desire have to be yours.

Risky Business

In order to win, a rider must be willing to take risks. Taking risks does not mean putting your life on the line and jumping fences that you and your horse are not yet ready for. I am not suggesting that death-defying peril is a necessary part of riding. The risks you must take are usually subtler ones that involve pushing yourself out of a comfortable rut and into more challenging activities.

Taking a risk may mean riding in a class that requires you to drop your stirrups or switch horses. It means trusting your instructor's advice and jumping a higher fence than normal, even if you are not sure you are ready to. It means branching out into other disciplines, such as eventing or stadium jumping, just to stretch your wings.

If you are not willing to take a chance, you will soon stop making progress in your riding. When that happens, you run the risk of riding on auto-pilot— doing the same things, riding in the same divisions on the same horses, over and over again.

Risk-takers, on the other hand, are constantly improving their skills, learning more about themselves and about their horses. They realize they will never know it all, but are willing to try anything. They enjoy the constant challenges of a demanding sport. That is what makes them successful.

Eliminate the Negative

So many things can distract a rider's focus and sap his will to win. These include:

- Nerves
- Laziness
- Insecurity
- Mousiness
- Timidity
- Desperation
- A bad attitude
- Whining

One or another of these negative attributes will surface in nearly every rider from time to time. The key is to identify the negative and meet it head on. If left unchecked, any negative trait will start to affect your performance.

Take *nervousness*, for example. Nerves can hamper your performance in different ways. Some people show their nerves by going too slowly. Some show them by going too fast. Some people rush through things when they are nervous. Some people will just never take a chance.

If you blow a class because you are nervous, take the time to ask yourself "Why?" Learn from your experience. Figure out what went wrong so the next time you can do something to correct it.

Be aware of how you are reacting. Identify what you are feeling. Then address the situation to offset the problems brought about by nervousness. (For more on dealing with nerves, see "Mental versus Physical Fear," p. 80.)

Desperation is another negative that can hurt you. If you are on a course at a horse show, and you spend the whole time trying to decide whether or not you are winning the class, you are not focusing on the job at hand.

If you are trying too hard, or if you "have to win," you are putting too much pressure on yourself and your horse. Allowing anything to distract you from your ride will negatively affect your performance.

Finally, beware of *generalizations*. Know what you are trying to do. Make your goal something specific.

In other words, don't try to find a "good distance." Don't try to have a "good round." Don't try to "look nice." These are too vague to quantify. "Doing well" is too general a goal. It is not easily identifiable when it happens. Instead, try to do specific things.

For instance, try to find the pace that will show you the correct distance or keep your heels down so you have good position. Pick one thing. Be specific and clear about what you want to work on. Then, set out to make it happen.

Nothing Beats Preparation

Confidence doesn't bloom in a vacuum. It is born of hours of hard work and practice. The key to confidence—the key to winning—is solid preparation.

If you have done everything you can to ensure a good result, even if you don't win, you should feel fine about it because you know you gave it your best shot. You have done your best. You trained your horse and mastered the riding skills required for that level. You arrived on time and ready to go. You stayed focused on the job at hand and rode as best you could.

You can't control many things, but you can control your preparation. You can control your foundation. You can control your understanding of the basics. The successful rider builds those so they are strong enough to carry him through the pressures of competition.

Ten Things I Hate About…

At the end of every show season, as we head for home after the finals, I make a list of the "Top 10 Things" that I wasn't satisfied with in my students' performances.

No matter how well my students ride, or how highly they place, there will always be at least ten things that aren't perfect. My list is just a way of keeping the training focused on what I want to work on next. It gives my students and me a manageable "homework" slate.

My list means I already know what I want to concentrate on for the next show season. Once my students master what is on the list, I will make another list of what they need to do.

I don't see the list as a litany of faults. Instead, I see it as a series of small, attainable, bite-sized goals. Making your own list allows you to see what specific things you have finally mastered. Ultimately, the list becomes your own private winning streak.

What Cost Winning?

Whether you ride on the local circuit or in the Olympic games, winning is never worth injuring yourself or your horse. Too few riders and trainers understand this, but it is true.

If you try to do too much too fast, or attempt something that is not feasible for a particular combination of horse and rider, then you are asking for trouble. That is when horses and riders get hurt.

If you push too hard for a single class or event and injure yourself, you run the risk of permanently ending your riding career. If you push your horse too hard, you literally risk his life. Know when to say "when." Never allow a prize to blind you to the risks involved in the larger picture.

Short-Term Winning = Long-Term Losing

When you consider the current climate in the horse show world, you soon realize the dangers of valuing winning over either your well-being or your horse's safety.

The very high level of performance that is expected of—and produced by—both horses and riders is astounding. The number of high-scoring rounds at today's horse shows attests to this.

In addition, there are more top-quality horse shows, finals, and special events available than ever before; many of which are far from horse-friendly.

Competitors find themselves showing their horses week after week, in the middle of large cities, at night outdoors under the lights, and in many other difficult or stressful situations. All of these factors, coupled with the considerable expense involved, create enormous pressure.

As riders, our job at every level of the sport is to determine ways to keep up with all the demands of competition without losing sight of the needs of our horses or ourselves. The issue of safe, humane competition requires careful consideration and thoughtful leadership. Winning at any cost is not the answer.

Remember: less is more. Too often, I see riders or trainers overworking their horses as they prepare for big events. While it is tempting to do more "just to be sure," or because there is a particular riding problem that you just haven't solved yet, it is imperative to reach for the best possible solutions with the least amount of wear and tear on our horses.

6.6 *Every rider, every groom, and every trainer should be aware of the distinction between medicating for the sake of the horse and medicating for the sake of winning.*

The horse that is overworked in order to win one class ultimately loses. He loses interest in his job. He loses respect for his rider. He loses enthusiasm for the show ring. And, if he is injured as a result of overwork, he loses the ability to ever win again.

The use of medication is another concern when examining the costs of winning. Too many competitors and trainers medicate all of their horses to the maximum levels. In reality, some horses would probably do just as well with less. More importantly, consider the very real probability that less work would result in the need for less medicating.

The field of veterinary medicine has made many recent advances in conditioning and maintaining performance. If these advances are used for the comfort of our horses, they are wonderful developments. If, however, they are used to sustain unnatural levels of work or performance, then they are really doing more harm than good.

While hard work, repetitive lessons, stress, and even medication are all realities in the rider's world, it is critical that we continually question what we are doing to our horses, and to what degree, at every step along the way.

We must not become casual or blasé at any point about what we ask our horses to do. These horses are our passion and our life. They deserve to be treated with respect. They are not disposable and must not be treated as if they are. Our responsibility is to stay true to ourselves and to our horses while we strive for results in our training and in the show ring.

Knowing When to Stop

A customer of mine once said that the trick to doing anything well is to always leave a little bit on the plate.

No one can become a world-class rider in one day. When training, do just as much as you or your horse can accept and understand comfortably. Then stop. Save the rest for another day.

I have often said that the most important goal when training a three-year-old horse is to have a four-year-old that is still sound and interested in learning.

The same concept applies to riders. The way I see it, the point of teaching a fourteen-year-old girl how to ride is not to have her accumulate as many ribbons as possible in the shortest amount of time. The real responsibility is to create a rider who still wants to ride and learn when she is older.

When schooling, if you are not sure that more work will benefit you or the horse, stop. Leave a little on the plate.

Rather than push for immediate perfection, aim instead for a sound, fresh, happy, trained horse and a sound, fresh, interested rider. Then you both can have a career that lasts as long as possible.

6.7 *The focus of riding is the horse—not the prizes.*

Maintaining Winning Standards

You must have a set of standards you hold yourself to whenever you work with animals. You and your horse will both benefit if you keep your standards as high as possible.

It should go without saying that our first priority as riders and trainers is the welfare of our horses. They are the focus of the sport. We get into riding because we love horses. We learn how to ride. We learn to compete. But, our enjoyment should never be at the expense of the horse. Sadly, we often *do* ride at the horse's expense.

Before you begin work with your horse, you should know your standards. You should already have a clear understanding of what you will—and won't— do before a particular situation arises. For example:

• I am unwilling to resort to using draw reins to bring my horse's head down.
• I am unwilling to ride or longe my horse more than two or three times in one day, even for a major event.
• I am unwilling to show a horse of questionable soundness, even if he is in the very beginning stages and I could "pretend" I don't know it is happening.
• I am unwilling to cheat.

6.8 *The only acceptable "unfair advantage" is putting in more effort, more preparation, and more work on the basics than anyone else.*

In my own mind, there is a line that I won't cross, even if it improves my chances of winning. Similarly, you must know your own boundaries. Learn to differentiate between healthy and unhealthy competition.

It is not healthy to be willing to do *anything* to ensure winning. Hurting the horse is unacceptable. So is hurting the other competitors. Giving yourself an advantage through bribery or drug use is absolutely out of the question.

Over-competitiveness hurts your horse. It hurts you. It causes you to hurt others. It can make you lose friendships and lose your self-respect.

Know exactly what you are willing to do and what you are unwilling to do. Try your hardest and ride to the best of your ability, but never lower your standards to please a judge or to get a ribbon.

Making the Best of a Bad Situation

No matter how minutely you plan or how thoroughly you prepare, you will occasionally find yourself dealing with an unexpected disaster.

Disasters almost always stem from errors in judgment. They can manifest themselves in a variety of ways. Some "disasters," like bad fences or bad rounds, don't count for much in the grand scheme of things. Others, like injuries, are much more serious.

Injuries, to me, are incredibly important. I am obsessive about soundness. If I have a horse that gets hurt from overwork, overshowing, overjumping, overschooling, or an overly emotional rider, it totally and completely devastates me—and it should. The feeling helps me ensure the injury does not happen again, but it is a heavy, hard lesson to learn.

When an injury occurs that you could have prevented, the best thing to do is learn from the disaster you created. In the future,

6.9 *Life is full of surprises. Some are more unsettling than others.*

the minute you start down that road, you should hear a warning bell in the back of your mind that tells you to stop.

When injuries happen (and they will happen) you must be a big enough person to shelve your competition goals in favor of your horse's well-being.

Handle all injuries with high ethical standards. Don't pretend the injury doesn't matter. Don't act as if the horse is fine and continue to go on in spite of things. Recognize what is happening. Respond to the situation. Always try to do the right thing—first for your horse, and then for yourself.

While injuries are at one end of the "Disaster Scale," bad jumps and bad rounds are at the other. Though a bad round is not the end of the world, you wouldn't know it the way some riders carry on.

Every rider occasionally takes a bad jump or has a bad round. For many riders, it happens all the time!

You might ride a line too slowly or take it too fast. You might chip a fence. You might try to do in five strides what should take six, or turn too suddenly or too late. Your memory might blank completely and make you forget what fence comes next. All you can do is try your best *during* a class and learn from your mistakes *afterward*.

6.10 *Desire, interest, and commitment are the most important contributors to a winning ride.*

When you have a bad round, you can beat yourself up for it, but that won't help you ride any better. A much more effective way to deal with the mistakes you make in the ring is to analyze what went wrong. Identify the specific problem areas you ran into. Plan how you will avoid them the next time you ride.

For all disasters that you encounter, use the past to build a better future. Don't dwell on past mistakes. Learn from them. Use them to become a better, more aware, more empathetic rider.

On the Money

You don't have to be rich to win. If you are not well-to-do, but riding horses and winning at horse shows is the most important thing in your life—and if you are willing to work as hard as you can and be creative in finding ways to make riding and showing possible—you will make it happen.

Several years ago, a student of mine decided she was going to aim to win the USEF Medal Finals. Her only horse was a very inexpensive one. She didn't have a lot of money to throw at showing. She and her mother did all their own work.

With her goal in mind, we devised a program and spread it out over three years. Everything we did during that time was geared toward getting her the experience she would need to win the finals.

When she got her chance—and she knew she would be able to afford only one—she was prepared to do what was necessary. She won. I believe that still can happen.

You can be successful in anything, whether you are rich or poor, short or tall, talented or untalented. Commitment matters more than anything else.

This is not to say that winners cannot be bought. Of course they can. Winners are bought every day of the week. You can buy a horse of great reputation, and a great reputation will definitely help when you enter the ring.

It is never easy to successfully compete against the wealthy and the privileged. But, *it can be done*. It is done over and over again, every day, in countless situations.

That is one of the wonderful things about this sport. You cannot completely buy success in the show ring. Even if you can afford the best horses in the world, you have to be willing to do a certain amount of work to win. You can't just strap yourself on and go for the ride.

Putting Competition in Its Place

Every so often it may be necessary for you to distance yourself a bit from the show ring and analyze your attitudes toward competition.

The show ring is nothing more or less than a venue where you can test yourself. While at home, ride your horse and take regular lessons. Work on particular areas of interest while you practice.

Then, go to a horse show and test your skills. Afterward, look at your scores or results. Evaluate your performance.

6.11 *If you find that your focus has somehow become more about riding well at shows than about simply riding well, a break from the show arena to spend some time rediscovering your passion for riding may be in order.*

Decide what old areas still need work. Identify new areas to start working on.

The cycle then begins again. After working at home, you go to horse shows and test your new skills. You reevaluate, and the process starts over.

Your attitude toward competition is an important part of this process. As you create a foundation, your riding gets better. As your skills grow, so does your confidence. As you build confidence, your attitude toward competition should improve. Ideally, rather than placing enormous weight on the outcome of a particular event, you will simply use it as one more tool to perfect your abilities.

The Fear Factor

Fear is not the same as nervousness. A rider who is afraid can't learn. If fear is an issue for you, don't ignore it in the hopes that it will just take care of itself. You need to address your fear honestly and confront it aggressively so it goes away.

For all practical purposes, this means that if you are afraid of riding, make sure your horses are quiet. If you are afraid of jumping, make sure your fences are tiny. If you are afraid of competing, enter only classes that you are easily capable of winning.

The best way to deal with fear is to arrange circumstances so the possibility of failure is extremely small. Then, as confidence grows and fear decreases, the degree of difficulty can gradually increase.

Mental versus Physical Fear

Mental fear and physical fear are two very different things. *Mental fear* is the fear of making mistakes. *Physical fear* is the fear of falling off and hurting yourself.

Though mental fear is usually less severe than physical fear, this is not always the case. All fear can build to a point where it inhibits the ability to enjoy riding.

More importantly, fear can actually cause a rider to do things that are unsafe. Mental fear can blind a rider to the difference between a fence that simply looks "scary," and a jump that is truly dangerous. Physical fear can make a rider clutch or grab at the horse, interfering with the horse's ability to jump or causing him to bolt in panic.

Nothing is more important than safety—and riding with fear can put both horse and rider at risk. This is why fear must be honestly and accurately addressed.

Fighting Stage Fright, Nerves, and Other Bogeymen

In many cases, mental fear manifests itself as nervousness or anxiety. Often, it is more noticeable in competition than at home. To combat it, try to recreate the cause of fear away from the show ring.

If a student of mine has a persistent problem with mental fear, I will look for an opportunity for him to face that fear at home. For instance, if he is jumping a course, and it is going well, I might yell, "I don't believe it! You're winning! Don't choke! Don't choke!" I might purposely distract him or try to get him to pretend he is at a horse show. In these cases, I want the student to tap into the part of himself that is terrified of making a mistake when it counts.

One of the best ways to conquer mental fear is to rehearse your "nerves" a little bit. Make yourself actually *practice* being nervous. Then you have the chance to learn to deal with it in the privacy of the home ring.

Another way to deal with nervousness is to consciously remind yourself that it is "only one class." Don't build the event up so much in your mind that it becomes an all-consuming, overpowering, stress-inducing obstacle.

Keep things as light as possible. Admit that your nerves might be an issue. Face your fear of making a mistake. Then, rather than allowing anxiety to sabotage your performance, work through it.

Finally, when dealing with show-ring jitters, realize that experience is the best teacher. In all likelihood, the more you compete, the less of an issue your nerves will become.

Facing Physical Fear

If a particular exercise has you suffering from physical fear, then you or your instructor need to change the exercise to something you feel capable of tackling. You can't learn if you are afraid you will hurt yourself.

The fearful student must have absolute faith in his instructor. At the same time, the instructor has to be aware of the student's concerns.

6.12 *For some students, trotting a ground-rail may be a huge confidence booster. Be honest about your fears and look for realistic ways to face them.*

6.13 *Fear is conquered through experience. The more experiences you successfully face as a rider, such as riding through streams and rivers, the more you will be able to know your abilities and keep your fears at bay.*

One of the best ways to develop faith is to start small. Use poles on the ground, cross-rails, tiny jumps, and quiet horses. If you think the horse is too fresh, longe him for a few minutes. Only do things that you know you and your horse are capable of. Each successful ride helps you develop trust in yourself, in your instructor, and in your horse.

What if I Fail?

Failure is inevitable. It is a normal, inescapable part of life. How should you deal with failure? The short answer is: learn from it, get over it, and move on.

Every successful rider you see has had his share of mistakes and failures—both in and out of the ring. No matter how carefully you plan or how diligently you practice, you will occasionally fall short of your goals. What matters most during these shortcomings are not the failures themselves, but how you face them.

When failure enters the picture, don't let yourself take things too seriously. Try to put things in perspective. Riding is *not* the cure for cancer, so lighten up. (In the grand scheme of things, does it really matter that you chipped in at the brush? Of course not.)

If you have had a spectacular failure, try to find some humor in the situation. Allow yourself to back away a bit and laugh.

Ultimately, if you are enjoying yourself as you ride, that counts for a lot. Ribbons and medals are not necessary to validate your enthusiasm for the sport.

If you find you are having too many failures, lower your expectations for a while. Give yourself a break. Jump lower. Go slower. Show less, or go to easier shows.

Sometimes dropping down a notch helps to combat failure. Regain your momentum and your confidence and then, when the successes begin to accumulate, build on them and stretch yourself again.

No "Pity Parties"

If you are struggling for success and are beating yourself up for doing badly, it is important that you listen when someone tells you not to be so hard on yourself. I don't have much time for those who want to wallow in self-pity. I can't stand the "Poor Little Me" syndrome, and all the spoiled, miserable, snotty-pants stuff that comes with it. It has no place in this—or any—sport.

If a student of mine fails and feels like it is his fault, or if he is being overly harsh with himself, I will step in and tell him to ease up a little. I will make a joke and try to gloss over the situation.

But, if a student messes up and tries to blame the instructor, the horse, the other competitors, the day, the judge, the course, or the jumps, I refuse to allow it. That is the worst kind of poor sportsmanship and I will not tolerate it.

I have seen too many instructors who are so worried about losing a customer that they end up teaching the rider to be spoiled. Don't allow yourself to blame a bad round on the heat, the course design, or the footing, when it was actually *your fault*. Don't expect your instructor to adjust your stirrups, clean your boots, or fetch you water.

Your instructor's responsibility is to teach his students to ride. It is not his job to cater to them or to teach them to make excuses for themselves.

Regardless of whether you are young or old, rich or poor, talented or not-so-talented, take responsibility for your own actions. If you make a mistake, pick yourself up, learn from it, and go on.

Set Yourself Up for Success

Success is a very personal concept. It can mean walking over a pole on the ground after you have been afraid to do it for months, or it can mean winning the medal at the Maclay, the USET, and the Washington Finals all in the same year. Success, like winning, means different things to different people.

Success is based on what you have done in the past. It is rooted in what you would like to do in the future. If you set realistic standards, then you will end up having a better shot at success.

Once you have had some success, you can build on it. You can choose another goal. You can stretch in a new direction. Then, hopefully, you will have new successes. Those successes will lead to others… and on, and on, and on.

Maintaining a Winning Perspective

It is so easy, as a competitive rider, to allow horses, riding, showing, and winning to become all-consuming. But, the reality is that a lot of things are more important in life.

It is very important that the goals you have are realistic ones and that you, as a result, are able to keep them in perspective.

Because success is so personal, it is vital that you create attainable goals. You are always better off creating too much success for yourself instead of too little. With every success, your confidence will bloom and you will end up going further, faster.

If you set goals that are too high, riding only becomes a lesson in frustration. Then, all you end up seeing is an apparently insurmountable obstacle far in the future. It can cloud your ability to recognize the small successes you experience along the way, and cause you to forget why you wanted to ride in the first place.

6.14 *Low expectations allow every rider to progress. Every person is capable of nearly limitless improvement, if given enough time.*

Keeping the Dream Alive

We all have pipe dreams. We all tend to have grand fantasies where we do "Important Things" and win big. Often, we think that we can do more than what is actually within our capabilities.

It is important, especially in the early stages of riding, to clearly separate your dreams from your goals. Your dreams can be as big and as bold as you want. But, take special care to keep your goals realistic.

Find someone that you trust to help you with these goals. Ideally, the person you work with should be your riding instructor. Talk with him. Tell him your dreams. Then tell him that you want the truth about the feasibility of ever achieving them.

Insist on the truth. Some instructors will try to sugar coat things for a favored client. If a rich customer who is 4' 2" and weighs 300 pounds says she wants to win the Medal Finals, any instructor who says, "Of course you can. You just need to buy these horses…" is taking advantage of the situation. In the end, unrealistic expectations are bad for everybody, especially the horses.

I am nothing if I am not honest with my students. I will tell them the truth about their chances of achieving their goals. To my mind, that keeps them from expecting unrealistic results and protects against later disappointments.

I am currently working with a rider who I would like to win the finals. She is a very good rider, but several things are working against her. She is very short. She is not thin. She is not an aggressive rider. And, she is not mounted to win.

These realities don't stop us from working toward the finals. We talk about the obstacles in her way. I tell her, "We will try to win. We will turn ourselves inside-out and try our best. Let's keep pushing and see if we can do it."

At the same time, we both understand that it is probably not going to happen. Most of the reasons why are beyond our control. We can't change her size. She can't afford to change her horse. But, that doesn't stop us from dreaming big.

Go ahead: dream big. As you set goals for yourself, however, be truthful. You know, within reason, what you can and can't do.

Your long-term goals may be too lofty for you to ever attain. Make them anyway. Then, set some short-term goals to get you started. Focus on the successes that the smaller, more realistic goals bring you. That way, you can keep on winning as you chase your dream.

Riding for Life

Many people begin riding because they love the time spent on and around horses. They envision many years of enjoyment on horseback. Too often, however, unrealistic expectations of how easy riding should be, poor instruction, an unhealthy emphasis on show results, or a simple lack of planning ultimately results in someone who "used to ride" but no longer does.

No riding discipline is an end unto itself. Instead, it is just one part of a lengthy, involved, fascinating, learning process.

The most important thing for you to gain from focusing on riding well is not a stash of trophies, but rather a tremendous sense of accomplishment from all of your successes along the way.

I believe that the process itself should sustain a rider's long-term interest. Show results, high-point awards, and medals are nothing more than progress markers. If success is measured in ribbons won, then the majority of participants in any division are setting themselves up for a short, disappointing riding career.

The way I see it, it is never too soon—or too late—to begin a life-long riding career. I have students in grade school as well as students with great-grandchildren.

It doesn't matter whether you want to ride competitively, professionally, or just for pleasure. If you challenge yourself to be the best horseperson you can possibly be, your enjoyment of the hours spent in the saddle will only increase.

Experience is always the best teacher, so create as many different experiences, with as many qualified, competent people as you can. Gain as much experience as possible in all aspects of the horse world. Learn as much as you can from people who work with horses for a living. Attend clinics, seminars, and other equine events. Ask questions of veterinarians, blacksmiths, and farriers.

Ride with as many different people as you can. Ride as many different horses as you can. Expose yourself to different styles of riding and different breeds of horses. Ride Morgans, Saddlebreds, Quarter Horses, and Tennessee Walkers. Ride hunt seat, Western, and saddle seat. Learn to drive. Try dressage, reining, or team penning. Go to the track. Anything you do with horses can be a learning experience.

Never stop learning. Continue to feed your "horse bug," and you will be well on your way to a lifetime of winning rides.

7

Choosing the Horse

Know What You Need

Because riding is a joint venture between you and your horse, choosing the right mount is important if either of you is going to perform well.

Competition Concerns

The great equitation horse is scopey, rideable, and tractable. He is physically capable of jumping lines that are long, short, tight, fast, or slow. He enjoys the challenges presented to him and carries his rider with ease.

Showing in the Hunt Seat Equitation, Hunter, or Jumper divisions can be interesting, challenging, exciting, and fun if you have a horse with the physical and mental propensity to be competitive. However, when good horsemanship is ignored and equitation is done badly it affects the horse negatively. It is easy to blame the horse for a bad round, but a bad rider or a bad instructor can easily make a horse afraid, make him miserable, or turn him into a joyless robot.

If you have a horse that is able to compete with ease—if he is athletic and willing—he can benefit

7.1 *Regardless of your preferred riding discipline, the ideal horse will allow you to spend time and energy improving your own abilities.*

7.2 *The "perfect horse" is one that can teach what you need to learn.*

greatly from competition. It will keep him interested and in shape. It can give him a purpose in life.

If, on the other hand, you have a limited horse, one that is unsound, nervous, or that really struggles with the physical requirements of the sport, I believe it borders on cruelty to ask that animal to compete.

Above all else—especially above any quest for a prize—consider your horse. The art and the challenge is to ride a horse that is capable of doing a good job, and to do it in such a way that he stays sound while both you and he remain interested and enthusiastic about the whole process.

Assess Your Needs

Before beginning your search, realize that the perfect horse does not exist. Every horse, like every rider, has both good points and bad.

Analyze what you will be asking of the horse. Take into account your own needs, as well as the requirements of your riding discipline. A horse that works well over 3' fences, for instance, may not have the same brilliance if asked to compete at the 3' 6" level. Likewise, a short-strided horse may be a capable schoolmaster, but will probably not be competitive in the show ring.

Look for a horse with strengths that can help you grow as a rider. Furthermore, realize that a trait one person might deem a weakness, another rider might consider a strength.

If you are just beginning to go over fences, for example, you want a horse that will calmly and quietly jump everything you point him toward. You don't want anything flashy or headstrong. You don't care whether the horse is pretty or not. You don't even need a horse that jumps with perfect style or correct form. You want an animal that knows his job and does it honestly, so your skills can progress.

Once you know something about riding, however, and are ready to start being competitive, you may discover that what were assets while you were learning become liabilities in the show ring. Competition demands a horse with a little more zing and a lot more flair and grace.

Remain Objective

There will probably come a time when you need to say goodbye to "Old Faithful" and move on to another mount that is more capable of helping you reach your goals. This often means that you must distance yourself emotionally when making your decision.

If you take an animal that is clearly unsuitable and try to make him into a hunter, jumper, or equitation horse anyway, you do him a serious disservice.

No matter how "attached" you are to your horse, if he has reached the limit of his abilities, it is preferable—and much more humane— to sell him and find another, rather than force him beyond his capacity.

7.3 When you are learning to jump, your horse's greatest asset is dependability.

10 ESSENTIAL TRAITS OF AN EXCELLENT EQUITATION HORSE

Since Hunt Seat Equitation judges the rider's position and ability, it takes an extraordinary horse that knows what is expected of him to allow the rider to excel within the division. The ideal equitation horse has many qualities. Above all else, he is:

1 *Scopey* He covers the ground well with a beautiful, free-flowing stride. When he jumps, he uses himself wisely and gives himself plenty of room to clear the fence.

2 *Rideable* His gaits are rhythmic and predictable. He readily turns left and right, responds to your legs, and respects the bit.

3 *Adjustable* The horse willingly extends or shortens his stride, increases or decreases his pace, allowing the rider to fine-tune the performance.

4 *Tractable* Nothing fazes him. He does not get "hot" or excited after taking a jump or two. He does not rush, shake his head, or twitch his tail in irritation.

5 *Capable* Equitation courses test horses with long lines and short lines. Some turns are tight. Some fences must be taken at a fast pace, while others are better taken slowly. The horse must be physically able to meet all these different (and difficult) challenges.

6 *Intelligent* He has a good brain and uses it.

7 *Honest* He knows what you want him to do and he does it.

8 *Confident* He might even be a bit cocky.

9 *Competitive* A really, *really* good horse works with his rider. He tries his hardest over every fence, every time.

10 *Sound* Soundness is absolutely critical at every stage.

7.4 *The honest, confident, capable horse is a true team player.*

Even if you do not intend to show in the Hunt Seat Equitation divisions, a horse that exhibits these qualities will always be an asset to you. Such a horse will allow you to focus on developing your own skills and will play an enormous part in improving your riding abilities.

The Horse Makes the Rider

When working on your equitation—your position, form, control, and coordination—choose a horse that will allow you to progress as a rider.

Quality First

As with everything else, buy the best quality horse you can find and afford.

For the Hunt Seat Equitation divisions, look for an athletic, willing horse that has a natural, comfortable, free-flowing stride. He should be absolutely sound and sane. He should enjoy jumping, be light on the bit, and be responsive to your legs. Since equitation classes are judged on the rider's performance, you want to be on a horse that is easy to ride, so you can look as good, as polished, and as capable as possible.

If you will be competing in the Hunter divisions, bear in mind that the horse is the focus of the judge's attention. Attractiveness and conformation are key elements in how your horse is judged. You want a horse that moves easily, with free, floating gaits. He should have a natural, low, sweeping stride that covers the ground efficiently. He should move forward from the shoulder with a minimum of knee action.

When the hunter jumps, he should lift his front legs at the same time. His knees come up, he stretches his head and neck forward, and rounds his back over the fence. He is alert, attentive, quiet, responsive, and mannerly.

Jumpers, in contrast, aren't judged so much on their appearance and attitude as they are on their athletic abilities. A jumper can hang his knees or lift his head over a fence. He can be ugly as sin and not particularly mannerly. Jumpers need to be able to take fences at angles and make sharp turns. The winning horse in a jumper class is the one that is most capable of getting the job done in the shortest amount of time.

A Custom Fit

You can see, then, the importance of choosing a horse that makes it easy for you to do your job as a rider. However, there is more to successfully pairing a horse and rider than simply finding an animal with the general qualities necessary to do what you have in mind for him.

7.5 A *If you are a long-legged rider, your ideal horse will have a round barrel to give you something to wrap your legs around.*

B *A rider with shorter legs will generally do better on a narrower horse that allows the legs to stretch down as far as possible.*

In the same way that you want a horse with training strengths that complement your experience weaknesses, you want a horse that is a good physical fit for you as well (figs. 7.5 A & B).

A general rule of thumb is that when your foot is correctly placed in the stirrup, the bottom of your heel should be even with, or just above, the bottom of the horse's belly. Your entire leg should be able to be clearly seen against the side of the horse.

If your foot hangs down below the horse's belly, you are probably too tall for the horse. If your heel is a considerable distance up on the horse's barrel, then the horse is probably either too tall or too wide for you.

Short riders often find that smaller horses suit them best. However, small horses tend to have shorter strides, which can be a liability in the show ring. If you are not a tall person, you must find a balance between a horse that fits your build and one that can easily handle the courses you want to ride.

Tall, thin riders have an aesthetic advantage over others, but a tall rider requires a horse with a complimentary build. Mounting a tall rider on a smaller horse tends to result in a top-heavy or overbalanced appearance.

If you are very tall, have long arms, or have a long torso, you will be best suited on a horse with a nice, long neck. A shorter rider will usually look more balanced on a horse with a shorter neck.

Don't ignore temperament when considering making a purchase. Again, choose a horse with strengths that complement, rather than duplicate, your weaknesses.

If you tend to be a timid rider, avoid timid horses. Instead, look for a horse that is honest, confident, and competent. If you are a nervous rider, opt for an unflappable mount.

Understand your own physical and mental makeup before you start horse shopping. Then you can tailor your search for an animal that highlights your strengths and minimizes your shortcomings.

When in Doubt, "Undermount"

I firmly believe that a rider must be undermounted in order to enjoy success. In other words, your horse should be *too easy* for you to handle. He should be the right size and shape and temperament for you. When you are learning how to do something, the horse should have lots of experience in that area.

If you are undermounted, then you will be able to put any worries about your horse out of your mind. You will be able to concentrate on developing the feel you need. You will be better able to focus on your lessons and on the goals you are trying to accomplish.

Get Help

Horse shopping is not something to do on your own. No matter how experienced you are, it is *always* a good idea to take someone knowledgeable along with you. It is also helpful to have someone whose opinion you trust watch you ride your prospect.

Ideally, your instructor will help you in your search. Your instructor's reputation is on the line every time you enter the show ring or ride with a group of people. It is in his best interests to have you well-mounted.

Your instructor is often able to look at the combination of horse and rider more objectively than you are. Listen to what he has to say and respect his opinion.

Don't let anyone talk you into a horse that you just don't like, however. You will be spending a lot of time, energy, and money on the animal you select. Weigh everyone's opinions carefully; then make a knowledgeable, informed decision.

8

Essential Equipment

Choosing Your Tack

Whenever you ride, whether you are at home or in the show ring, your tack should be clean and in good condition. It should fit both you and your horse (fig. 8.1). If your tack is fitted correctly, and if your horse is conditioned and worked properly, you don't need a lot of extras.

My attitude toward my equipment is the same as it is toward the rest of my riding. I get the best quality equipment I can find. But, where the horse's training and well-being are concerned, the philosophy of "less is more" still applies.

8.1 *Think of your horse as an athlete. Your tack is the athletic equipment necessary for your "team" to perform at its best.*

Whenever possible, reduce. Very few "gadgets" are necessary in a well-balanced, deliberate, knowledgeable riding or training program.

Rather than loading up on a lot of cheap (and unnecessary) equipment, focus on acquiring top quality, well-crafted essentials. Your tack will last longer, wear better, and be more comfortable for you and your horse.

The Saddle

Excellence in riding is only possible when both horse and rider are comfortable, conditioned, and free of pain. Regardless of your level of expertise, good performance is directly related to good saddle fit. The most talented horse and rider team in the world won't be able to reach their full potential with a saddle that doesn't fit.

A correctly fitting saddle should make you feel balanced, even if it is not on a horse. You should also be able to easily put your legs in the correct position when sitting in it. I recommend a close contact, forward seat saddle with the least amount of knee rolls or blocks possible. This allows the rider to feel the horse more and have security through the leg and base without sacrificing that feel. I also like a saddle with a very flat seat. I feel it keeps the rider closer to the horse's back.

A poorly fitting or badly constructed saddle can lead to a wide variety of problems. It can cause sore or pinched shoulders, pressure points, bruised backs, and even nerve damage. An improperly fitting saddle can interfere with the horse's natural movement and balance. In some cases, saddle fit is directly responsible for such behavioral problems as bucking, rearing, bolting, balking, and head tossing.

Determining whether or not a saddle fits a particular horse and rider is an acquired skill. Unless you have considerable experience in saddle fitting, you should take someone knowledgeable along with you as you saddle shop.

The Long View

A horse's body changes as he matures, as his muscles develop, and as his conditioning improves or diminishes. Be aware of how your horse's physiology relates to the equipment he carries.

Pay attention to what your horse is telling you. If he suddenly starts throwing his head, twitching his tail, or having difficulty picking up a particular lead, check your tack. See if your saddle fits as well as it used to, or if discomfort is the underlying cause of your horse's symptoms.

Your saddle is a significant investment—not only in terms of money, but also with respect to the amount of time you will spend in it. You will ask your horse to perform athletically while wearing it. You will count on it to keep you secure while galloping and jumping. You will literally trust it with your life.

Saddle Pads

"Less is more" certainly applies to saddle pads. If you have a well-fitting saddle and a minimum of padding the horse will be most comfortable, and the rider will have the most feel.

When showing, I use a small, white, synthetic fleece saddle pad. It is understated and nearly unnoticeable. For schooling, I use what I call "baby pads." These are thin, white saddle pads of quilted material like in a baby-mattress pad. They're easy to clean, look neat, and absorb sweat. The baby pad goes directly on my horse's back.

On top of the baby pad, I use a rubber pad made by ThinLine. These are very thin and dense, and designed to absorb the most shock possible. They offer my horse's back a great deal of protection without a lot of extra bulk.

I don't use pommel pads, bounce or lift pads, or gel pads—as a rule, I steer clear of any extra padding between my saddle and my horse.

The Girth

I prefer leather, shaped girths with elastic on one end. Elastic on one side, rather than both sides, allows just the right amount of "give." I find that the shaped girth is more comfortable behind the horse's elbows, which helps eliminate chafing.

Most horses don't need extras, such as fleecy girth covers. Some, however, are thin-skinned and require them. Add covers on an as-needed basis.

The Bridle

The English bridle is made of leather. The leather may be rolled or flat and should be the same color as the saddle. The bridle must include a browband, noseband, and throatlatch (fig. 8.2). Snaffle and kimberwicke bridles use a single set of closed reins. Pelham and double bridles require two sets of closed reins.

8.2 *The bridle holds the bit in place so the reins can provide a direct line of communication to the horse.*

When the bridle is correctly fitted to the horse, the cheek buckles are in line with the horse's eye. The browband is the same color and made of the same material as the rest of the bridle. It is wide enough to allow the ears plenty of room. It should be broad, flat (not padded), and understated.

Bits and Bitting

The bit is the rider's most obvious and most direct means of control. Bits may use either direct or leveraged pressure to influence the horse.

The bit should be wide enough to comfortably fit in the horse's mouth without pinching his lips or cheeks. A correctly fitting bit is about half an inch wider than the horse's mouth.

Acceptable bits include the snaffle, the kimberwicke, the Pelham, and (on occasion) a combination of snaffle and curb in a double bridle. Unconventional bits may be penalized at the judge's discretion.

Martingales

The martingale is an optional piece of equipment in jumping classes. Martingales are not allowed in flat classes.

Martingales may be either running or standing.

- The running martingale is shaped like a "Y." It is designed for use with a snaffle bit. The base of the "Y" goes between the horse's front legs and attaches to the girth. The reins pass through metal rings at both forks of the "Y." When the horse raises his head, the rings exert downward pressure on the reins, encouraging him to flex at the poll and yield to the pressure. When using a running martingale, your reins should have "stops" on them to limit how far they can pass through the rings (figs. 8.3 A & B).
- A standing martingale attaches to a cavesson noseband, rather than the reins. A strap runs from the noseband between the horse's front legs to the girth. The strap passes through a neck loop that encircles the horse's neck. The standing martingale prevents the horse from raising his head above a certain level. It keeps him from tossing his head and avoiding the bit. It also restricts the horse from falling forward out of frame or pulling against the rider (figs. 8.4 A & B).

8.3 A *The rings of a running martingale should reach to the base of the horse's neck, just in front of the withers.*

B *"Stops"on the reins keep the running martingale's rings from interfering with the bit.*

8.4 A *The standing martingale attaches to the cavesson of the bridle (shown here with a Pelham).*

B *The correctly fitted standing martingale just reaches the horse's throatlatch when he is standing still.*

Boots and Wraps

At home, for schooling, my horses work with polo wraps on their front legs to help protect and support them. If a horse needs specific boots in front, or boots or polo wraps on his hind legs, they are used on an as-needed basis.

I'll add bell boots in addition to polo wraps for turn-out and longeing. If the horse starts bucking and playing, bell boots prevent heel grabs.

8.5 *In the show ring, classical hunter attire never goes out of style.*

Boots and wraps are not allowed in the show ring in Hunter divisions. In the equitation ring, while boots are allowed, I always use the minimum amount necessary. If boots are needed, my preference is for open-front galloping boots and hind ankle boots. Boots should only be used to protect the horse's legs from injury. I find the current trend of using weighted hind boots in the Hunt Seat Equitation division reprehensible.

Boots are also allowed in the jumper ring. Again, I prefer to use open front boots, which allow the horse to feel any rubs he may have on the course.

What to Wear

The two general rules of thumb for all riding attire are that it must be neat and it must be clean.

As with everything else associated with correct riding, form follows function. Every article of clothing, every piece of equipment, and every piece of tack at one time served a purpose in the hunting field (fig. 8.5).

For instance, the high collar shielded the rider's neck from abrasions from tree branches. The stock tie could be removed and used as a tourniquet or bandage, and the stock pin made an excellent impromptu bandage holder.

Today, much of our show clothing has historical significance, rather than an immediate usefulness. It is all a part of hunt seat riding's grand tradition.

Still, neatness, tidiness, and cleanliness never go out of style. Your riding attire should include the following:

Helmet

Always ride with a helmet. *Always.*

Helmets are not just for use in the show ring. They are an integral part of riding safety. You will never be "so good" that you don't need a helmet.

Helmets protect you in several ways. They keep you from getting a severe cut if you hit something like a jump standard or a horse's hoof during a fall.

They also help absorb a fall's force of impact and protect your brain inside your skull.

According to the United States Equestrian Federation (USEF) Rule Book, all competitors in Hunter, Jumper, and Hunt Seat Equitation divisions must wear an ASTM/SEI certified riding helmet. In addition, all junior riders must wear a certified riding helmet while mounted at any place and at anytime on horse show grounds.

For practice, any approved helmet will do. For the show ring, however, black velvet is the traditional choice. In order to be effective, your helmet must be clean, ASTM /SEI certified, and well-fitting.

Boots

Always ride with either boots or paddock boots. Your boots should be made for riding. They should have good arch and ankle support, and a good heel (fig. 8.6). As with everything else in your riding, invest in the best quality boots that you can afford.

With few exceptions, children showing in the Small and Medium Pony divisions should show in paddock boots and jodhpurs. Tall boots may be worn by older children and in the Large Pony divisions, and they are in order in all Horse divisions.

In the show ring, it is critical that your boots are always freakishly clean. Knock the mud and dust off of them before you get on the horse. Keep them clean, dirt-free, and shining. In my opinion, nothing speaks more clearly of a student's respect for his riding, his competition, and his instructor than when he has clean, shiny boots.

Breeches

Breeches should be a neutral color that complements you and your horse. The breeches you wear in competition should be understated in the extreme. Rather than wearing flashy breeches, use great riding to draw attention to yourself.

8.6 *Boots should fit tightly to your calf and come all the way up to the bend in your knee. When wearing them, you should be able to flex at the ankle and ride with your heels down.*

8.7 Breeches are not necessarily required for lessons. For practice, many students prefer to wear jeans and chaps, or jeans and half chaps.

It goes without saying that your breeches should fit well and be scrupulously clean.

If I have a rider who is not yet totally comfortable riding in show clothes, then I have that student practice in boots and breeches. When the rider is able to do the same ride, regardless of whether he is wearing boots and breeches or chaps, then it doesn't matter whether he wears boots and breeches for practice anymore (fig. 8.7).

Practicing in boots and breeches is the best way to emulate the "feel" of show day. The more variables you can take away from your practice rides, the more consistent your performance will be when it counts.

Shirt

For practice and lessons, the shirt you wear is largely a matter of personal choice. T-shirts, polo shirts, and oxfords are all acceptable as long as they are clean, well-fitting, and neatly tucked in.

For women, show shirts should have a stand-up or "ratcatcher" collar. Whether or not the shirt has sleeves is a matter of personal preference and depends largely on the climate where you will be competing. Men should wear a traditional shirt and tie.

Shirts should be light and neutral—no gaudy colors. Any print or pattern should be minimal. Avoid anything that might distract from you and your horse's performance. If in doubt, remember: classic elegance and tastefulness are always appropriate for the show ring.

Jacket

For the horse show, one jacket of top quality is better than two of lesser quality. It should go without saying that your jacket should be clean and well-fitting, tasteful, and understated.

Riding in a jacket for practice and for lessons is not necessary, although, as with boots and breeches, it is a good idea to get used to the feel of wearing a jacket when riding at home.

Spurs

As a general rule, I like riders to wear spurs, even if they never have to use them (fig. 8.8). Wearing spurs means that you always have the option to use them if you need to.

With spurs, the rule of "less is more" applies (see p. 19). Wear the smallest spur possible. I like my students to start with a short Prince of Wales spur with no rowel.

If you think you need more spur—one that is longer or roweled—examine your rationale. Too often, using a harsher spur falls under the "Quick Fix" category. When using spurs, as with any other training aid, make sure you consider your training program. You may need to change your program rather than your equipment.

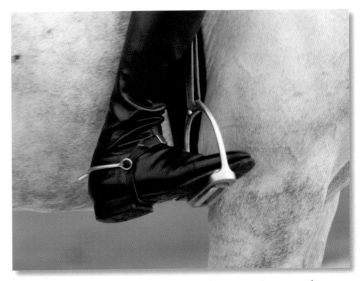

8.8 *Correct spur adjustment. The spur does not point up or down, but is parallel with the heel of the boot.*

Crops, Sticks, and Bats

Learn the proper way to carry a stick or crop (fig. 8.9). Hold the handle in the palm of your hand. The top of the handle should be by your thumb. There is no "loop" around your wrist.

Practice riding with a crop. Be comfortable holding it in either hand and switching it from hand to hand.

If you don't need the crop while you are riding, don't use it. But, if you don't have one and need to reinforce a leg cue or encourage impulsion, you will have to stop what you're doing, dismount, and go get it.

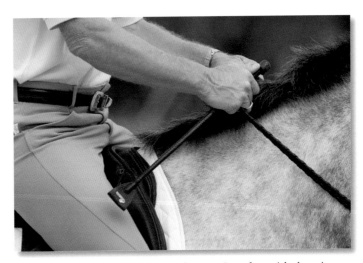

8.9 *When held correctly, the crop does not interfere with the reins. The end of the crop goes back toward the horse's hindquarters, not straight up and down toward his shoulder.*

With any training aid, always consider what is best for the horse. Stopping in the middle of a lesson to pick up a piece of equipment is rarely beneficial to the training process.

JUDGE'S CARD
WHAT RIDERS WEAR

HIGH MARKS / NO FAULTS

- Overall appearance is workmanlike and tidy.
- Rider is correctly attired, wearing clean, well-fitting hunt clothes and boots.

COMMON FAULTS

- Jacket, shirt, and breeches too small or too large.
- Wrinkled or dirty clothing.
- Poorly fitting or dirty boots.
- Inappropriate riding attire. (If the rider is incorrectly dressed for the ring, the judge or the show management may eliminate him and excuse him from competition.)

MANDATORY RIDER ELIMINATION

- Failure to wear approved protective headgear.

9

Perfect Position
Understanding and Developing
the Physical Aids

Fundamentals of Position

According to the United States Equestrian Federation (USEF) Rule Book, *equi-tation* is defined as "that position that allows the rider to perform a function with the least amount of energy."

Equitation *is* position. Proper position is the foundation—the common denominator—of all good riding.

The ideal overall position is one where the rider exudes a general work-manlike appearance. He is calm, poised, and confident. He gives the impression of being able to ride with complete control through any situation that might present itself.

The rider must not be stiff or unyielding while mounted. Correct position allows you to move in harmony with the horse.

If your position is correct, your eyes are up, your shoulders are back, your leg is underneath your body, and your heels are down. The calf of your leg is slightly behind the girth, in contact with the horse. At the walk, sitting trot, and canter, your body is a couple of degrees in front of the vertical. When posting the trot, galloping, or jumping, your body is inclined slightly forward, about 30 degrees inside the vertical (figs. 9.1 A & B).

9.1 A *Sitting near the vertical at the walk, sitting trot, and canter allows the rider to influence the horse's balance and forward motion.*

Angle Awareness

Perfecting your position is simply a matter of controlling *angles*. An angle is formed when two straight lines join together. *Closing* the angle brings the two lines closer together. *Opening* the angle takes the lines further apart.

A rider's body has four angles of significance: the ankle, the knee, the hip, and the elbow.

- The *ankle angle* is formed where your foot meets your leg. A closed ankle angle means your heels are down: you have brought your foot closer to your shin. Another way to say "Heels down" is "Close your ankle angle." Both phrases mean the same thing.
- The *knee angle* is formed where your calf connects with your thigh. Bringing your leg back underneath you closes the knee angle somewhat. When posting, the knee angle opens and closes in rhythm with the horse's trot.
- Your *hip angle* occurs where your upper body attaches to your thigh. Closing your hip angle means leaning forward. Opening your hip angle means leaning back or approaching the vertical (sitting up straight).

9.1 B *Inclining the body about 30 degrees forward when posting, galloping and jumping enables the rider to follow the horse's forward motion.*

- The *elbow angle* is formed by your upper arm and forearm. Bending the elbow, or bringing your hands up, closes that angle. Bringing your hands down or straightening your arms opens it.

The Four Fundamental Parts of the Rider

When talking about the position of the rider on the horse, I separate the body into four different parts, starting at the bottom and working my way up.

The four fundamental parts include:

- Legs (from the knees down)
- Base (from the knees to the hips)
- Upper body (everything above the hips, including the head)
- Hands and arms

THE LEG: *Building a Solid Foundation*

When addressing your position, start at the bottom. Whether I am judging, teaching, or working on my own riding, I always begin with a consideration of leg position. You can't have a good position without a good leg (fig. 9.2).

9.2 *A good leg: the foot in the iron; the toe is turned out slightly; the stirrup is angled slightly on the foot, allowing it to hang perpendicular to the horse; the leg is in position, in contact with the horse.*

Start with the Stirrup

Good leg position stems from correct stirrup placement. The iron should be just at the ball of the foot (where the toes attach), or even a touch in front of it. Correct position developed to give the rider maximum security combined with maximum flexion of the angles in the legs.

If you ride with the stirrup *ahead of* the ball of your foot—on your toe—you run the risk of losing your stirrup. You may also have a less stable base of support.

If you ride with the stirrup *behind* the ball of your foot, then you have less flexibility in your ankle and knee and less depth of heel (figs. 9.3 A–C).

Adjust the stirrup iron at an angle on your foot so that when your toe is slightly turned out, the stirrup hangs straight and the iron is perpendicular to the horse's side.

Heels Down!

Let your stirrups firmly hold your feet while you sink into your heels. Relax your ankles and let your weight push your heels down. Your heel should be as deep as possible.

The further your heels are down and the more your leg is around your horse, the tighter and more secure you will be when riding. Dropping your heels lowers your center of gravity. Keeping your heels down is the beginning—the essence—of a long, tight leg.

Back, Down, and In

Once your feet are set correctly in the irons, then you can concentrate on your legs.

9.3 A *Correct position of the foot in the iron.*

B *Riding with the stirrup too far out on the toe increases the odds of losing a stirrup and makes for less security on the horse.*

C *When the stirrup is too far back on the foot, the rider lacks flexibility in the ankle and loses depth of heel.*

The legs should be underneath you. They shouldn't be kicked out in front of you, which can throw you behind the horse's motion. Your legs also shouldn't be pushed too far behind you, which will cause you to tip forward onto the horse's neck (figs. 9.4 A & B).

Contact with the horse should be evenly maintained, with your weight distributed down through your whole leg.

Stretch down around the horse. Imagine stretching your legs longer and longer. Keep as

9.4 A *When the leg is too far forward, it pushes the rider's body and balance too far back.*

B *If the leg is too far back, the rider's entire body topples forward.*

much of your lower leg as possible around the horse. Keep the leg tight, but be sure you do not pinch with your knee.

You should be able to feel that the angles in your leg are bent. The ankle angle is closed. The knee angle is also bent. That means your heel is down with your leg back beneath you.

Think "back, down, and in": bring your legs *back* underneath your body, push them *down* toward the ground, and bring them *in* or curve them around the horse's sides. Strive for a feeling of a deep, tight leg enveloping your horse.

When your leg is in position on the horse, it is tight and secure. The horse's motion—whether moving forward at a particular gait or jumping an obstacle—doesn't move the leg out of position.

Determining Stirrup Length

Stirrup adjustment is critical. When first adjusting your stirrups, sit on the horse with your feet out of the irons, and let your legs hang relaxed (fig. 9.5). Pay attention to where the bottom of the stirrup iron falls in relation to your leg. This will help you maintain a consistent, correct stirrup length if you ever have to quickly change horses or tack.

Your stirrups should be longest for flatwork. That is when you will want to have the longest leg possible and be in a position to influence your horse more.

For jumping and galloping work, however, you *follow*, rather than *influence*, the horse's motion (see "To Follow or to Influence?" p. 122). You want to be able to

9.5 *Correct adjustment for normal stirrup length. When the foot is out of the stirrup, the iron should just touch the ankle bone.*

9.6 A *Normal stirrup length: knee and ankle angles are moderately closed. This is a good, solid position for basic work over fences.*

B *Jumping length: stirrups are slightly shorter for forward, faster work. The knee and ankle angles are more closed. The thigh is more parallel to the ground. The entire leg is more compressed.*

C *Flat length: stirrups are slightly longer for flatwork. Notice the angles of the knee and the ankle are considerably more open than in previous lengths. This allows a longer leg that can influence the horse more.*

hold yourself in a balanced and closed position, interfering with the horse as little as possible.

In general, the higher the jumps are, the shorter your stirrups need to be. Shorter stirrups enable you to get off the back of the horse and follow his motion in the air over the fence (figs. 9.6 A–C).

You may prefer to have your stirrups even shorter for showing. Many people find that riding with boots and breeches can change the way a ride feels. Often, riding with stirrups one hole shorter can help.

Once you have perfected your position and developed some muscle memory, you will be able to adjust your stirrups according to what feels right. In the early stages of your riding, however, what feels right is not always correct.

In general, if you have a question about stirrup length, you are better off with a stirrup that is a little bit too short rather than too long. There is nothing worse for your position than constantly reaching for your stirrups.

Exercises with Stirrups

● ADJUSTING YOUR STIRRUPS

Practice adjusting your stirrup with your foot in the iron. Taking your foot out of the iron can compromise your safety in case your horse bolts or shies or spooks or stumbles. You want to be as secure as possible while you actually make the stirrup adjustment.

Schooling

1   Hold your reins in the hand on the opposite side as the stirrup you want to adjust. (If you will be adjusting the left stirrup, hold the reins in your right hand.)
2   Keep your feet in both stirrup irons. Keep your leg in position and your heels down, but don't put much pressure on the stirrup during the adjusting process.
3   Adjust the stirrup leather. Use your free hand in front of your leg to pull up the end of the leather. Make the adjustment and reposition the leather so the buckle doesn't gouge into your thigh. Throughout the process, maintain your position as much as possible (figs. 9.7 A–C).

The Point

Practice until you can adjust your stirrups at the standstill and at the walk. Remember: safety is the top priority.

Adjusting your stirrups isn't a big deal. It certainly doesn't require bringing the training session to a screeching halt while you ride into the center and dismount or have your groom or trainer wait on you hand and foot. Quietly, quickly, and discreetly make the adjustment and then continue with the ride.

● PICKING UP DROPPED STIRRUPS

Dropping your stirrups and picking them up again is important to master. For one thing, it is an acceptable equitation test for a judge to require. Safety reasons are even more important than horse show results, however.

9.7 A *Take a little weight out of one stirrup. Hold the reins in one hand. Reach in front of your leg with the other hand. Pull the buckle toward you, out away from the horse.*

B *Put the buckle where you want it. Use your index finger to push the tongue of the buckle into the "keeper hole."*

C *Pull down on the bottom strap, bringing the buckle up flush against the stirrup bars.*

Schooling

1 At the standstill, take both feet out of the stirrups. Without compromising your overall position (pay close attention to your hands!), put your feet back in the stirrups as quickly and as correctly as possible. Practice this until it becomes second nature.

2 When you have mastered dropping and picking up both stirrups at the standstill, practice it at the walk, the trot, and then the canter.

3 Practice dropping your stirrups and picking them up over jumps.

4 Practice dropping just one stirrup and picking it up again.

The Point

Merely getting your feet back into the stirrups isn't the most important part of this exercise. The point is to recover your stirrups without ruining your position.

Knowing that you can quickly regain a lost stirrup can help you greatly in an emergency. If the horse bolts or shies and you drop your irons, you have already practiced and acquired the skill of being able to pick the stirrups back up again.

Exercises without Stirrups

Working without stirrups serves one of two purposes. It can either help make your leg longer, or it can help make your position stronger.

Generally speaking, when working without stirrups, I like my students to cross the irons over the horse's withers (fig. 9.8). This keeps the irons out of the way—it keeps them from banging the student's ankles and smacking the horse's elbows. If you are going to be practicing without stirrups for some time, you might want to go so far as to pull the stirrup leather down so the buckle doesn't hit you in the thigh.

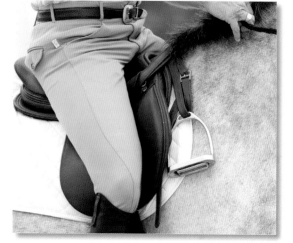

9.8 *Stirrups crossed properly for work at home.*

● DEVELOPING THE LONGER LEG

When you are doing *sitting* work, riding just a few degrees in front of the vertical, you can influence the horse's balance and motion.

To be most effective, try to make your leg as long as you possibly can at the walk, sitting trot, and canter. In sitting work, you bring your leg out from the saddle and wrap it down around your horse. Your thigh becomes almost perpendicular to the ground as you stretch your leg.

Schooling

1 Keep your feet in your stirrups as you correct your position at the walk.

2 Drop your stirrups. Try to make your leg as long as possible. Stretch your legs down and wrap them around your horse.

3 Pick up the sitting trot. Feel how your body reacts as the horse changes gaits. The natural inclination is to want to pull your leg up to hold yourself on the horse. Instead, think about continually stretching your leg down, lengthening it, and bringing it back underneath you.

4 After a while, walk and correct your position. Work to maintain your position as you transition from the trot to the walk. Don't let the horse sink out from underneath you.

5 Go from the walk to the sitting trot again and again. Practice circles, serpentines, and turns. Focus on lengthening and stretching your leg down.

6 When you are comfortable at the sitting trot, practice riding without stirrups at the canter. Periodically transition back to the walk or sitting trot and correct your position.

The Point

Doing sitting work without stirrups helps to develop a long leg. You want to be able to maintain that length of leg at any gait and through transitions from one gait to another.

In this exercise, as you go to a faster gait—from the walk to the sitting trot, or the sitting trot to the canter—the natural reaction is for your leg to become short. In reality, however, you are working to train yourself to go against that natural reaction (figs. 9.9 A–C).

Be patient. The ability to maintain a long leg on your horse is an acquired skill.

9.9 A *Working without stirrups to stretch the leg longer at the halt…* B *at the sitting trot…*

C *and at the canter.*

9.10 *Posting without stirrups makes the leg stronger. The legs should be in the same position they would be if your feet were still in the irons.*

● DEVELOPING THE STRONGER LEG

When you ride at the posting trot, and when doing galloping and jumping work without stirrups, you ride in two-point contact with your seat out of the saddle. In these instances, your main goal is to make your leg stronger. Therefore, instead of stretching your leg toward the ground and making it longer (as in "Developing the Longer Leg," p. 116), you ride with your leg in the normal position as if you had stirrups.

Schooling (Beginner)

1 Put your leg in proper position at the walk.
2 Pick up a working trot. Post with your leg in correct position (fig. 9.10).
3 When you feel your leg fall out of position, walk again and correct it before picking up the posting trot again.

Schooling (Intermediate)

• Transition from a posting trot to a canter and back again.
• Canter in galloping position (two-point) with your legs correctly placed.
• Ride at a slow gallop without losing position.
• Jump over low rails.

Schooling (Advanced)

• Transition from the posting trot to the gallop and back again.
• Jump over higher fences.

The Point

In this exercise, you work at perfecting your balance and position so you can support yourself and be strong on the horse.

As you work at posting, galloping, and jumping, your leg should be the same length as it would be if you were riding with stirrups. The point is to make your leg stronger—to build muscle memory and strength that will enable you to maintain your position with or without stirrups.

If, at anytime, you feel yourself lose your position, transition to a gait where you are comfortable. Sit in the saddle and correct your leg. Then, start working with two-point contact again.

JUDGE'S CARD
SCORING STRENGTHS AND FAULTS IN LEG POSITION

NO FAULTS

Every judge wants to see riders with good leg position. Ideal position includes all of the following:

- Leg maintains close contact with the horse.
- Rider is secure and confident.
- Heels are down.
- Knees are relaxed and bent.
- Ankles are flexed slightly in.
- Stirrup iron is correctly placed at an angle on the ball of the foot.
- Stirrups are adjusted to the correct length, allowing the rider's leg to wrap around the horse, while keeping the knees bent and the heels down.

COMMON FAULTS

- Stirrup irons incorrectly placed on the feet (feet are either too far "home" in the stirrups, or the stirrups are only on the rider's toes).
- Stirrup length is too long. Rider is reaching for the stirrups.
- Stirrup length is too short. Rider has insufficient length of leg.
- Lack of leg control: legs swinging, heels up.
- Legs in incorrect position: too far back or too far forward.
- Uneven stirrups.
- Twisted stirrup leathers.
- Not enough weight in the heels.
- Losing contact with the saddle or losing a stirrup.
- Insecure position.
- Grabbing or clutching at the horse.
- Foot extremely rotated, toes out.

THE BASE: *The Seat of Good Riding*

The base includes everything from the knee up to the hip. A long base, like a good leg, is important to good riding. Your goal is to wrap your leg and thigh around the horse as much as possible.

The purpose of good base position is the same as for good leg position. A good base allows you to be tight to the horse (fig. 9.11). The more your thigh is long and your leg is down around the horse, the more secure you will be. Both your leg and your base give you security on the horse.

A long, balanced, tight leg and base are how you stay on. When positioned correctly, your leg and your base put you right in the middle of the horse—secure, tight, and able to deal with anything.

Relax the Knee

You should have tension, or contact with the horse, through your whole leg. The contact should be evenly distributed from your hip to your heel. What you don't want to do is concentrate the bulk of your contact at the knee.

Knee-pinching occurs when you bring your thighs up and squeeze in with the knees to hold yourself on the horse. This common fault provides a false sense of security.

Gripping with your knees does not lengthen or strengthen your leg. It actually makes your leg on the horse become shorter. It raises your center of gravity and takes your weight out of your heels. Ultimately, you are holding on just with your knees. Knee-pinching results in an unbalanced, insecure rider.

Instead of pinching, you need to *relax* your knee. Allow all of your weight to come down through your leg. Once your leg is as long as it can possibly be, then bring the whole leg into contact with the horse.

Create tension through your whole leg. Ideally, you will have a tight leg—and a tight base—all the way down. Your weight and your contact will be evenly distributed through your thighs, your knees, and your calves.

Hips and Heels in Line

Your base and your legs work together. They function best when they are balanced beneath you.

For good, effective position, your hips and heels should be in line with each other, and your knees should be bent enough to provide effective shock absorption.

If you ride with your leg jammed out in front of you with your foot pushing against the stirrup, you will actually push your seat up and back in the saddle. This gives you less security. It also straightens out your knee angle and creates a rigid, unbalanced leg.

Bringing your thigh back and underneath you helps your seat stay in the center of the saddle. It allows all of your weight to drop down through your ankles, increasing your security and stability.

You can, however, bring your thigh *too* far back. When that happens, your upper body automatically topples forward, ahead of the horse.

If your leg is forward, your balance and body is too far behind the horse's motion. If your leg is too far back, it will force your body balance out ahead of the motion. If your leg is underneath you, your body is balanced. Keeping your hips and heels in line will help keep you balanced.

9.11 *A good, strong base brings security. The hip angle is open, placing the rider just in front of the vertical. Head, hips, and heels are in a straight line.*

Base Position

Sitting in the saddle is all about your seatbones, not your tailbone. When you are mounted, you want to feel your seatbones in the saddle.

Your center of gravity is through your buttocks and your legs. You need to sit on your seat, but if you use *only* your seat, your leg will come up. Ideally, you will use your leg and your seat together.

Stretch your weight down into your heels. Then drop your weight down into your seat. Have your weight distributed as deeply as possible all the way around your horse.

9.12 A *Following the horse's motion in the posting trot. Hip angles are closed. The rider's body follows the horse, but does not inhibit the horse from stretching and moving forward.*

B *Influencing the horse's balance at the sitting trot. Hip angles are open, with the rider sitting on the seatbones, but also balancing down through the leg.*

To Follow or to Influence?

The more you are centered and even on the horse, the more comfortable your horse will be. Depending on the gait, you will either *follow* the horse's balance or *influence* it (figs. 9.12 A & B).

If you ride at the posting trot or the gallop, or if you are jumping, you are *following* the balance. When this happens, your body inclines forward slightly and moves forward with the horse. The horse moves ahead with energy and carries you along with him.

When you follow, you use your crotch more than your seat. When posting or working in two-point contact, focus on feeling your crotch more than your seat. They are entirely different things.

If you are riding at the walk, sitting trot, or canter, you are *influencing* the balance. In those cases, you sit straight, just a few degrees in front of the vertical, and encourage your horse's balance to come up and back to meet yours.

Your position subtly affects the horse's balance or carriage. The lighter the horse is in front, the more he can use his hind end. Influencing the horse's balance enables you to focus more energy in his hindquarters, allowing for more collection and a greater concentration of power.

When you are influencing the horse's balance and motion, you should be able to feel your seatbones in the saddle.

You don't ever want to collapse the small of your back and let your tailbone become part of the equation. Collapsing at the waist allows your tailbone to drop down into the saddle. It rounds your back and throws your seat forward instead of keeping it underneath you. Riding in such a position makes it impossible for you to correctly influence or follow the motion.

Angles for Following

In general, whenever you are following the horse's motion, you are riding in two-point contact. In two-point contact, you do not use your seat to influence the horse. Instead, you follow the horse's motion and allow him to carry you forward.

Two-point is both a position and an exercise. As an exercise, the reins are "bridged," or held in one hand while the other hand holds the mane to balance the body. Two-point position gets its name from the two points of contact the rider has with the horse: each leg provides one "point." When riding in two-point position, the reins are held normally (figs. 9.13 A & B).

In two-point, your upper body is angled about 30 degrees inside the vertical. You should feel as if you are *slightly* forward. When two-point is done correctly, your weight is evenly balanced over your legs rather than being carried in your shoulders.

When riding in two-point contact, your angles are closed:

- Your weight is driven down into your leg, creating an even deeper heel.
- Your knees are bent, lifting your seat out of the saddle and acting as shock absorbers. If you shorten your stirrups to a jumping length, your knee angles will be even more closed.

9.13 A *Two-point as a balancing exercise. The reins are held in one hand, while the other hand helps support the rider.*

B *Riding in two-point position. All weight is balanced through the heel and through the base. The rider is not balancing on the horse's mouth and maintains a beautiful line of contact from bit to elbow.*

- Your hip angles close as you incline your body forward to follow the horse.
- Your elbow angles close as you shorten your reins and move your hands up the horse's neck in order to maintain contact and control.

Base Function

The function of the base is security. Since your base starts at the knee, it affects all of your riding, and not just the parts that involve sitting on your seat.

In two-point, even though your seat is out of the saddle, your thighs are still on the horse. When you are in two-point, your weight drops down through your leg. Your base stretches as long as it can in the thighs. Then, you hold that position tight.

When jumping, a secure base helps you. Even though your seat is a little out of the saddle, your weight still stays down through your base. The more secure your thighs are, and the longer your base is while you are jumping, the more secure you will be over the fence.

Certain situations, however, require you to follow the horse with three points of contact, using your seat in the saddle as an additional balancing and driving aid (fig. 9.14). A *three-point following position* is useful for rollbacks, tight turns, and other instances when you want to slow the horse's forward motion without compromising his impulsion and power.

Base Practice

As you do your seated work, an awareness of your base and your seat in the saddle will help develop additional strength and balance.

Pay conscious, focused attention to balancing in your seat, as opposed to balancing on your hands. Be aware of the need for an independent seat—one that does all the balancing for you.

The best practice for a strong, secure base is working without stirrups. The more you ride without stirrups, the more secure you will get. The more secure you are, the more relaxed you will become.

Ride without stirrups frequently. Mentally isolate your base—from your knee to your hip—and pay attention to how it feels at the various gaits. Focus on stretching your base longer. Work on getting your base tighter. Your goal is to be relaxed while seated securely in the middle of the horse.

9.14 *In three-point position, the seat remains in the saddle. The hip angle is closed and the rider's body inclines about 30 degrees inside the vertical.*

JUDGE'S CARD
BASE BASICS

NO FAULTS

A great base that gives the rider security and stability includes:

- Close contact with the horse when necessary.
- Correct hip angle for each gait.
- A supple, balanced seat.
- Effective, quiet use of the seat.
- Relaxed, flexible knees.
- Hips in line over the heels.

COMMON FAULTS

- Riding against (ahead of or behind) the motion.
- Stiff or rigid riding.
- Sitting off-center.
- Gripping with the knees.
- Losing contact with the saddle.
- Excessive or unnecessary motion.

THE UPPER BODY: *The Balance of Power*

The upper body comprises everything above the hips, including the head. The hands and arms are separate body parts that—ideally—operate independently. However, poor position or lack of upper body control affects the hands and arms as well. A perfectly positioned upper body that is strong and secure in the seat is a great aid to developing independent hands.

9.15 *Correct upper body position includes a slightly arched back while sitting on your seatbones. It is supple—never stiff.*

The ideal position for your upper body depends upon whether you are influencing your horse's balance or following the motion.

Riding to Influence

Remember, every time you do sitting work, riding at the walk, sitting trot, or canter, you influence the horse's balance. The more you can affect the horse's balance with your weight and the position of your upper body, the less you need your hands and your arms to achieve the same thing.

Your back should be slightly arched (fig. 9.15). To achieve the correct arch, think in terms of "lifting" your chest and your stomach. With your seat fixed in the saddle, lift yourself up through your spine. Push your chest and stomach out in front of you until your upper body approaches the vertical.

Hold your body just inside the vertical. Lean a few degrees forward, rather than sitting straight up and down.

The Physics of Influencing the Horse

During sitting work, your upper body and your base are in position right over the center of the horse. Holding the upper body tightly in position allows you to get more reaction from your horse in response to your legs.

Stretching yourself up and back also allows you to lift your horse's balance up off his front end and shift it to his hind end.

When influencing the horse's balance, you are, in essence, riding the hind legs forward first and lifting his front end up and back. You are moving what was balancing on that front end (or perhaps, on your hand), up and back onto the horse's hocks.

The more the horse's hocks are underneath him, the easier it is to get him to lift himself up and go where you ask him.

Influencing the horse's balance does not mean hauling back on the reins in an effort to force him to redistribute his weight to his hind end. All balance work should be light and soft. You are training the horse to pay attention to what your upper body is doing. The horse should always be lighter at the end of a lesson than he was at the beginning.

Angles of Influence

When doing sitting work and focusing on influencing the horse's balance, think in terms of open angles.

Your leg is as long as you can possibly make it, so your knee angles are open.

You are sitting straight on the horse with your upper body just a few degrees in front of the vertical. This position opens your hip angles.

You should have a straight line from your elbow to the bit in the horse's mouth. Since your upper body sits straight up on the horse, in order to achieve the straight line through your forearm to the bit, your elbow angles are slightly open as well.

The only angle that remains "closed" is your heels. Heels down—always.

An Exercise for the Upper Body

● STRETCHING FORWARD AND BACK

Stretching your upper body up and back will help you get comfortable holding the arch in your back while changing your hip angles (figs. 9.16 A–C).

Schooling (Beginner)

1   At the standstill, concentrate on lifting your chest and stomach up. Then push your chest and stomach out, or forward. Hold the position while you breathe normally.

2   Bend at your hips (rather than at your waist) and lean forward. Lean as far toward the horse's neck as possible. Hold yourself there.

9.16 A *Lean as far forward as possible over the horse's neck without losing the arch in your back.*

B *Lean back without affecting the rest of your position.*

C *Then, lean back as far as safety and physics allow.*

3 Without hitting the horse in the mouth, sit up and regain your position.

4 Bend at your hips (rather than at your waist) and lean back. Bring your entire upper body back behind the vertical. Hold yourself there.

5 Maintaining the position of your base and legs as much as possible, stretch yourself up and back. If your horse is quiet, you may even go so far as to rest your head on his back near his tail.

Without hitting your horse in the mouth, sit up and regain your position.

Schooling (Intermediate)

• Do the exercise at a walk.

Schooling (Advanced)

• Practice the exercise at a sitting trot.

The Point

Putting your upper body behind the vertical is a great exercise for building strength. It gives you more strength behind your hands (if you are taking your horse up and back) and your legs (if you are asking the horse to go forward).

Eyes Up!

Your body follows your eyes (fig. 9.17). Therefore, your weight will subconsciously move toward wherever you look. If you start looking down, you will collapse your upper body forward and down as well.

Focusing your eyes on a fixed point helps keep your upper body in optimum position. Holding your eyes up also helps you develop a better overall feel for your position.

9.17 *Keeping your eyes up, looking at a point straight ahead of you, makes it easier to maintain your upper body position.*

Common Upper Body Faults and How to Fix Them

Riding ahead of the Motion

A common fault riders make when following the horse's motion is trying to balance their weight out through their shoulders. This results in a rider who is ahead of the horse, rather than following him.

Do not throw yourself up on the horse's neck. Riding too far forward makes you insecure and top-heavy (figs. 9.18 A & B).

To Correct the Fault

Open your hip angles. Keep your weight down through your legs. Remember to keep your hips and heels in line. Practice riding in two-point position at all gaits without using your hands on the horse's neck for balance.

9.18 A *What not to do: here, the rider is ahead of the horse's motion. Note the extremely closed hip angles. Too much of the rider's weight is carried in his shoulders. This position actually pushes the horse's balance down in the front.*

B *Riding ahead of the motion over a jump causes you to straighten your legs and balance more in your stirrups than in your heels. It is often directly responsible for making the horse hit the jump with a front leg.*

Roached Back

Maintain a slight arch in your back. This ensures that you work from your seatbones and not from your tailbone.

A roached back occurs when you lose the arch created from lifting your chest and stomach (fig. 9.19).

To Correct the Fault

Inhale deeply and lift your stomach and chest. Feel how that creates a slight arch in your lower back. Hold the arch while breathing normally.

Riding Too Stiffly

Some riders have all the grace of a brick. They may even have perfect position, but are so rigid, stiff, and unyielding that it is painful to watch them ride. Though you want to be able to hold yourself in position on the horse, you need to be able to do it with fluidity and grace.

Riding is about moving naturally in time and in tune with the horse. Overly stiff riding doesn't do anyone any good.

To Correct the Fault

Get more comfortable on the horse's back. Riding without stirrups will help loosen you up. A few longeing lessons may also help to soften and supple your riding.

9.19 *What not to do: the roached, or rounded back causes the rider to sit on the tailbone, as opposed to the seatbones.*

HANDS AND ARMS: *Fine-Tuning the Feel*

Soft hands make a soft mouth. Stiff hands make a stiff mouth. Dead hands make a dead mouth. Whatever kind of hands you ride with, that is the kind of mouth that you will create in your horse.

Your hands and arms should be soft and supple. Suppleness is the foundation of feel. You want to feel the horse's mouth without hanging on it.

9.20 *Independent hands are tied to having an independent seat. You cannot have one without the other.*

9.21 *Correct hands. A straight line runs from the elbow to the bit. Hands are just in front of the withers. Elbows are slightly bent, just in front of the body.*

Aim for Independence

Independent hands and an independent seat are the goals of every serious rider (fig. 9.20). When you achieve them, your balance is through your legs and base. You don't use your reins for security or to keep you on the horse. Instead, you use your hands and arms for communication.

When your leg is long and tight, when you have done your work without stirrups, when you have done your two-point work, and when you are totally secure on the horse, *then* you will have independent hands.

The ideal, of course, is to develop soft, supple, quiet hands that operate independently of the body. Such hands allow you to subtly communicate with the horse. They maintain constant, light contact. They influence without interfering.

The Line to the Mouth

One of the most important elements of developing good hands is the concept of maintaining a straight line to the horse's mouth. You should be able to draw a line from the bit through the reins to your hands, then through the forearm straight to your elbow (fig. 9.21).

If you are going to break that line, you are better off breaking it above the line rather than below it. In other words, raising your hands so the reins move the bit up into the corners of the horse's mouth is preferable to dropping your hands and pulling the bit down on the bars of the mouth (fig. 9.22).

Looking for the Ground

Ideally, you want to be in a position to influence the corners of the horse's mouth. You want to ride in such a way that will allow him to accept your hands. The ultimate point of good hands is to teach the horse to reach out and down with his neck—to look for the ground.

If you are influencing the corners of the mouth, when the horse accepts your hand, it will be easy to relax on his mouth. His head will either remain where it was or reach out and down. He will maintain self-carriage and continue to work forward (fig. 9.23).

Conversely, whenever you cause the bit to work on the bars of the horse's mouth, the horse's head will

9.22 *What not to do: the hands have separated and are working down, below the line from the elbow to the horse's mouth. This works the bars of the mouth and results in a tense, resistant, uncomfortable horse.*

9.23 *When the horse accepts your hand, he will continue stretching himself and maintain his balance and his forward motion, even when you release all tension on the reins.*

9.24 *What not to do: working the bars of the horse's mouth results in grudging over-flexion and inhibits the horse's forward flowing movement.*

come up. Even if he flexes his neck somewhat and *seems* to accept your hands, his head will come up as soon as you relax tension on the reins (fig. 9.24).

This is the opposite of your goal of having a horse that stretches forward. Therefore, it is very import-ant to maintain a straight line to the horse's mouth. To do so, supple arms and hands are essential.

Soft, Straight, and Supple

When working on position, remember to keep your hands soft. Soft hands are sympathetic hands. They are following hands. They come from the rider being supple in the elbow and shoulder. They come from the rider being empathetic—feeling what the horse wants and being sensitive to it. Having soft hands is a far greater asset than having hard hands in perfect position.

When your arms are supple, they are relaxed at the shoulders and the elbows. The entire arm is elastic, relaxed, and capable of following the horse's mouth, head, and neck.

As the horse moves forward into the bit and establishes contact, you should have a stretching feeling in your elbows. Slight pressure is necessary in order to keep the contact. Keep the line from bit to elbow straight, but remain relaxed, soft, and supple.

Perfect Hands

The rein should come from the horse's mouth and pass between the third and little fingers of both hands. The excess rein goes up your palm and comes out at your thumbs. The *bight*, or loop of excess rein, falls to either side of the horse's neck. (Ideally, the bight falls to the outside when riding on a circle.)

9.25 *Light contact and a willing horse make for a relaxed, comfortable ride. Note the straight line from elbow to bit.*

When holding the reins, your hands should be right next to each other, but not touching. Thumbs are on top, just inside the vertical, with palms almost facing.

Close your fingers around the reins. Don't clutch at them with fists of steel. But don't hold on to them so lightly that any little movement the horse makes pulls the reins through your hands.

Keep your wrists straight. Remember: you want a straight line from your *elbows* through your *wrists* through your *hands* through your *reins* to the *bit* in the horse's mouth.

Say to yourself, "Hands together, just inside the vertical…fingers closed around the reins…"

I tell my students this over and over. I use it as a catch phrase and as a means of "brainwashing" them. Then, when we are working on something else, if their hands get out of position, all I have to do is say, "Hands together…" and they mentally fill in the rest of the phrase and correct their position.

Making Contact

Contact is often a misunderstood concept among riders. Contact is about establishing a light, consistent means of communication with your horse through the reins (fig. 9.25). It is not about pulling on the reins to create an artificial frame or to hold the horse's head in a particular position.

Think of contact as "relaxed tension." The horse should be working forward so that he reaches out with his head and neck. Ideally, he actually pulls a little on your hands.

You can only feel the horse's mouth if there is no loop in the reins. If the reins have a loop—or slack—in them, there is air between your hands and the bit. At that point, contact has been lost and you cannot feel the horse's mouth through the reins.

Contact involves putting your horse enough in front of your legs that he is pulling *slightly* forward. The key to the concept is that the horse reaches forward and creates the contact with you. You do not pull backward and force contact with him.

When done correctly, contact allows you to have a light feel of the horse's mouth without influencing the rest of his body. In other words, you want to be able to feel the horse's mouth without affecting his balance, without slowing him down, and without making any part of his body—including his mouth—stiffen up in resistance.

Correcting with Resistance

Having soft, supple hands does not mean that you give up control.

If your horse is doing something with his head that you don't want, such as tossing his head, holding his head and neck too high, or whinnying, soft hands allow you to use your reins as a means of communication and control.

When the horse does something you don't like, simply increase your contact. Close your fingers against the horse's mouth and put steady pressure on it. That is "resisting the mouth."

When the horse relaxes and accepts the hands, you also relax your hands and reward him (figs. 9.26 A & B).

Resisting the mouth means closing against the mouth with your fingers but *not* pulling against the mouth with your arms. It is *not* taking the horse's mouth by force. It is simply applying corrective pressure until he responds to it.

The same concept also applies for rewarding the horse. When you are riding with light contact, as soon as he does something that you love, relax your fingers and make the contact even lighter. Don't throw the contact away completely, but let up on it enough that the horse feels a slight release.

Whether you are correcting or rewarding the mouth, remember to maintain steady contact. The contact never stops. It only varies by degrees.

9.26 A *Follow the line to the horse's mouth, even if he raises his head. Closing the fingers resists the mouth a little. It corrects the horse, but does not try to pull his head down.*

B *As soon as the horse gives to the bit, all resistance in your hands stops.*

The Semicircle of Rein Aids

To best understand the various rein positions, imagine that the horse's bit is the axis of a circle. A line extending to the right and left of the horse bisects the circle.

The resulting semicircle extending back toward the rider covers the area that can affect the bit. Pressure may be applied to the bit from a variety of directions and angles, depending on the placement of the rider's hands and arms (figs. 9.27 A–D).

The rider sits straight on the horse, holding the reins in both hands. The reins are even, with light contact on the horse's mouth. This is the "Base Position."

Applying pressure to a particular rein can affect the horse in several different ways, depending on where the pressure falls on the semicircle. A short explanation of the position, feel, and use of a given rein aid follows.

- Opening Rein   The opening rein is the basic first step when teaching a horse to follow a rein and be guided by pressure on the bit.

  Using a right opening rein from the base position would mean holding the right rein to the right, away from the horse's neck. This "opens" the rider's right side and applies pressure to that rein. The horse's nose follows the pressure out to the right. Then, his body follows his nose, turning to the right as well.

  An opening rein is used when teaching young horses to turn. Also, if you are jumping a line and your horse shifts to one side, an opening rein to the opposite side is a powerful tool.

- Direct Rein   A direct rein to the right involves bringing your right hand toward your right hip.

  Two direct reins applied at the same time are usually used to bring the horse back, balance him, get direct flexion, and slow the horse down.

- Indirect Rein (in front of the withers)   A right indirect rein *in front of the withers* involves moving your right hand toward *your* left hip.

  Indirect reins displace weight. The right indirect rein in front of the withers displaces the horse's weight from one shoulder to the other. If you are using a right indirect rein in front of the withers, moving your right hand toward your left hip displaces the horse's weight from his right shoulder to his left shoulder.

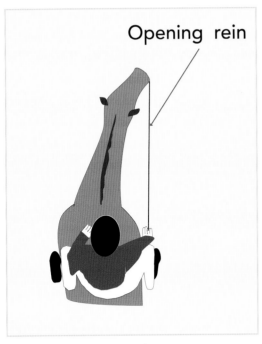

9.27 A *The right opening rein.*

B *The right direct rein.*

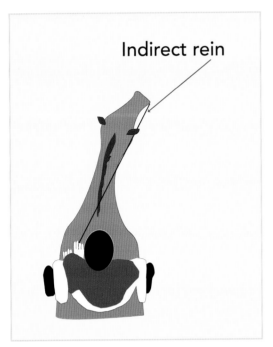

C *The right indirect rein.*

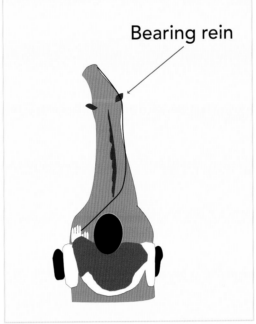

D *The right bearing rein.*

- **Indirect Rein (behind the withers)**   A right indirect rein *behind the withers* begins with a right opening rein. You then move your right hand toward *your horse's* left hip.

  This indirect rein's purpose is to displace the horse's weight from his right shoulder to his left hind leg.

- **Bearing Rein**   The bearing rein is similar to the neck rein in Western riding. When turning the horse to the left, a right bearing rein assists the left rein. It exerts slight pressure against the horse's neck on the right hand side, keeping the horse's right shoulder from falling out and keeping his body on track.

  Too often, the bearing rein is used incorrectly, and it becomes an exaggerated indirect rein instead. It actually ends up bending the horse in the opposite direction of what was intended. This results in an uncomfortable horse that is behind the rider's motion and center of balance. The bearing rein should be used only at the most advanced levels.

An Exercise for Practicing Position

When working on your position, it is best to have somebody on the ground to help you. If you don't have another person, you can use a mirror to evaluate your progress. Ultimately, however, the point is to be able to feel your position.

JUDGE'S CARD
HAND POSITION

NO FAULTS

Excellent, independent hands include the following:

- Placement just in front of and above the horse's withers.
- Angled 30 degrees inside the vertical. Thumbs up.
- Hands slightly apart. Wrists straight. Elbows slightly bent. A straight line runs from the bit to the rider's elbow.
- Quiet, supple arms.

COMMON FAULTS

- Poor or incorrect position.
- Stiff or rigid riding.
- Contact on the reins is too loose or too tight.
- Dropping a rein.
- Rough, uncontrolled hands.
- Using the reins for balance or to maintain the rider's position on the horse.
- Holding onto the saddle.
- Jerking on the reins or catching the horse in the mouth.

● FOCUS ON FEEL

This exercise is simple in concept, but requires frequent revisiting throughout a rider's career. It is a good way to attune your body and your mind to the feel of correct position. In it, you simply focus on the "feel" of correct position one piece at a time.

Preparation

Assume the correct position. Have someone on the ground help you, if possible. If you are just beginning to work on position, do the exercise at a standstill or the walk. Eventually, however, do it at all gaits and while jumping a fence.

Schooling

1 Look at a point straight ahead. Remain in correct position throughout the exercise. Become hyperaware of your *legs*. Pay attention only to your legs. Feel what your legs are doing to maintain the correct position.
2 After a while, move your awareness to your *base*—your upper thighs and seat. Feel how they move and work to maintain the correct position.
3 Next, move your focus to your *upper body*. Feel how it moves and balances when in correct position.
4 Finally, focus on your *hands and arms*, and feel what they are doing.

The Point

If you make good position a habit—if you train your body to have an innate feel for correct position—then you will be better equipped to tackle new challenges as they arise.

Deliberately make yourself aware of how the various parts of your body feel in a particular position. Good position is the best possible base from which to work.

Correcting Poor Position

Unfortunately, many people do not cultivate correct position when they begin riding. Many factors, including lack of interest, insufficient coordination, and poor instruction can contribute to faulty position.

Poor position can be fixed, but it takes work. Often, it takes longer to unlearn a bad habit than it does to instill a good habit "from scratch."

The only way to correct what has become a habitual poor position is to dedicate time and patience. You need to allot specific time to correct specific problems. At first, you will have to constantly adjust your position in order to build a new good habit.

If you have a problem with your leg position, the first step is to get your legs correctly in place while at a walk. Once your legs are in position, trot a few steps. Then walk and correct your leg. Then go back to the trot. Do this over and over and over.

Be patient with yourself as you develop new muscles to correct a particular position fault. Work at it until the correct position becomes such a habit that it "feels wrong" if you ride differently.

Muscle Memory

The more attuned you are to the way correct riding feels, the more you will be able to influence and control your position. Trying to constantly monitor every nuance of your body, however, is an exercise in futility. Fortunately, good position can become just as much a habit as bad position.

In the early stages of learning to ride correctly, continually reassessing and fine-tuning yourself is necessary until your muscles become used to working and moving in a particular way. But there comes a point when your body remembers what you have taught it. "Muscle memory"—a sort of auto-pilot, self-correction—kicks in.

Muscle memory helps you maintain the position you have practiced without requiring much conscious thought.

In other words, you become comfortable with your leg back. You become comfortable with your heels down. You become comfortable riding with a bend in your elbow. Then, when your horse acts up, or you are in a competitive situation, your muscle memory and your habits maintain what you have worked to perfect.

10

Riding Factors

Identifying the Intangibles

Regardless of your preferred riding discipline, the point of training is to teach the horse to push himself from his hind end and move forward while staying straight and light. He should "look for the ground" through the bridle, reaching out and down with his neck. He should accept your hands. He should be well schooled for his job and maintain an alert, willing attitude (fig. 10.1).

Several factors contribute to the art of riding. These include:

10.1 *The horse that moves off a light leg and responds to a light rein is a joy to watch and ride.*

- Maintaining lightness
- Developing a feel for the horse
- Perfecting and coordinating your aids

When you add jumping over fences to the mix, fine-tuning your performance means you must also develop an awareness of such things as line, pace, and distance.

Since these critical elements are intangible and not easily quantified, they often fall into the "You'll Know It When You Do It" category and, as a result, can be difficult for riders to master.

When you want to better understand a particular part of your riding, you must first identify where to concentrate your efforts. Don't use the "blanket approach" and try to work on everything at once. Decide what you want to improve. Isolate that area of your riding and spend some time focusing only on it.

This chapter contains some simple exercises to help increase your proficiency in the essential intangibles.

10.2 *Lightness involves knowing how the horse responds to a given aid and then using just enough to get a reaction. It means always looking for a way to do less.*

Developing Lightness and Feel

From the moment you get on your first horse—as soon as your instructor tells you to keep your heels down or corrects the position of your hands—your work on developing lightness and feel begins.

No one masters lightness or feel right away. No one expects you to. You must immediately start developing an awareness of the concepts, however, if you ever want to ride effectively, effortlessly, and invisibly.

Lightness Defined

Working a horse with *lightness* means using the least amount of an aid possible. It doesn't matter whether the aid in question is your hands, your legs, your seat, or your weight. The object of good riding is to always use the least amount of force or pressure necessary to get the result you want (fig. 10.2).

Riding with lightness does not mean that you are ineffective. If you use too little of an aid, your horse receives no direction—and nothing happens.

Lightness leads to responsiveness. The lighter you are as a rider, the less resistant your horse will be.

Finding Feel

Feel relates to both the rider and the horse. "Riding with feel" means knowing what is going on with the horse underneath you. It means being aware of aspects of your course without looking directly at them. It means having a sense of where your horse's feet are landing. It also involves being mindful of your position without looking to check it.

Feel is a developed awareness of the horse. It is the ability to connect with specific areas of the horse's mouth through the reins. Feel allows you to identify the horse's individual footfalls and determine what parts of his body are at rest or in motion at any given time.

Many instructors teach visually. They will instruct until a rider's leg *looks* good, or the horse *looks* flexed, or the horse *looks* like he's jumping with correct style.

But the rider can't see how he looks. He can only know how something feels.

Riding is based on feel. You want to feel what is happening beneath you and be able to accurately assess it. Developing feel will help you assimilate the good habits that lead to instinctive riding.

Though some riders have an instinctive sense of the horse, I believe *feel* is a skill that can be learned, just as you can learn to keep your heels down or learn to post on the correct diagonal.

Visualization can help develop feel. While your horse moves forward, visualize where his feet are falling as you feel the rhythmic pattern of his gait.

You can learn to feel straightness—whether or not your horse's hind feet are following exactly in the tracks of the front feet. You can learn to feel when your horse is moving at a normal, 12-foot stride. Furthermore, a feel for your position can help you determine that your hip angle is closed, or that your leg is correctly placed under you.

JUDGE'S CARD
AVOIDING EXTREMES

When the rider is doing things right, his position complements the horse. Then, both horse and rider move in harmony with one another. Riding with feel is the antithesis of riding with exaggeration.

In my experience, anything exaggerated or extreme on a horse is probably wrong. If I am judging and a rider does something obvious that draws attention to itself, more often than not, that "something" is wrong.

If the rider's leg is too far out, too far back, too far down, or too far in, it is an exaggeration. The same is true if someone is riding with a swayed back instead of a slightly arched back. Overemphasizing any one aspect usually tips the balance and takes the rider's position from correct to wrong.

The "Goldilocks Factor": Feel and Lightness Combined

Feel and lightness are closely related to each other. In order to be an effective rider, you need to learn to feel just the right amount of hands, legs, seat, and weight. The more you can feel what that right amount is, the more lightness you will have in your riding.

To better understand the relationship, remember the story *Goldilocks and the Three Bears*. Think in terms of "Not Enough," "Too Much," and "Just Right."

For example, if you want to bring the horse back but are too light with your rein aids, you will not get any reaction. If, however, you apply too much pressure with your hands and reins, you will only feel the horse's resistance.

You need to find a point where the horse willingly accepts the aid and responds to it. When that happens, feel how light your aid is. Feel your horse willingly accept it. Remember that feel for future reference. Then reward the horse and move on, maintaining that level of lightness in your riding.

Exercises for Developing Lightness and Feel

● DEVELOPING THE LIGHT LEG

A horse that readily moves forward in response to the rider's leg aids is an asset to your riding. A dull and heavy horse lacks forward motion and makes riding a chore.

The following exercise can help your horse pay attention to you while simultaneously keeping your leg aids light.

Schooling

1 At the halt, look ahead. Choose a point to ride toward.

2 Relax pressure on the horse's mouth and allow him to go forward. Lightly close your legs against his side.

3 As soon as the horse responds and moves forward, relax and reward him. He is doing exactly the right thing.

4 If the horse doesn't react to a light leg, immediately cluck and use your stick to reinforce your leg. Use the cluck and the stick together. When the horse responds and goes forward, stop clucking, stop using the stick, and relax your leg (figs. 10.3 A & B).

10.3 A *Relax your reins and close your leg. If the horse doesn't move forward, cluck and use your stick.*

B *Relax all pressure as soon as the horse responds.*

5 After a few strides, bring the horse back to the halt.

6 Repeat the exercise. Every time you start again at Step 1, choose a different point to ride toward.

The Point

Remember to relax your reins before asking the horse to move forward. Use a light leg aid, even with a dull or heavy horse. If the horse responds, relax. If he doesn't respond right away, use a cluck and a stick rather than increasing your leg pressure.

The cluck and the stick teach the horse to pay attention and to be responsive to a light leg. Consistent exposure to this exercise will ultimately result in a horse that moves forward and responds quickly to a light leg.

● "GOLDILOCKS" BACKING-UP

Though this particular exercise focuses on getting a feel for the amount of hand pressure needed to get the horse to back up effectively, the principle applies to a variety of situations. You can use the Goldilocks Factor to help develop a feel for lightness in all your aids.

Keep in mind, however, that the amount of pressure required to get a horse to respond to an aid varies. Over time, as you practice this exercise, the

10.4 A *Not enough: if you have contact with the horse's mouth, but don't do anything, the horse won't do anything either.*

B *Too much contact causes resistance, even if the rest of your position is correct.*

C *Just right: instead of resisting the rider, the horse has accepted the pressure on the bit and is yielding to it.*

horse should become more and more responsive, and your aids should become lighter and lighter.

Schooling

When working on the flat, bring the horse to a halt.

- **Not Enough** Do nothing with your hands and try to back your horse. Nothing will happen. That's the "feel" of not enough hands.

- **Too Much** If you grab on to the horse's mouth and are very dead and heavy on the reins, chances are he will immediately resist you. He may set his jaw or raise his head. He might even brace back against his front feet and refuse to move. That's the "feel" of too much hand pressure causing resistance.

- **Just Right** Experiment between varying degrees of "Not Enough" and "Too Much." Find the level of contact that puts pressure on the horse's mouth without creating resistance to that pressure. When you find that point, keep the pressure steady and wait (figs. 10.4 A–C).

  Wait until the horse accepts your hand and relaxes. You will feel him relax his jaw, his poll, and his hocks. This puts him in a position to back up.

The Point

You won't know what level of lightness is the right amount unless you practice and see for yourself. You must know what "Not Enough" and "Too Much" feel like in order to cultivate a feel for what is correct.

● PUSH, DON'T PULL

When schooling at home, your goal should always be to get your horse working longer, lower, and lighter. You want him to work with his muscles stretched out, as opposed to working with his muscles tight or bunched together.

Just as you would stretch your own muscles before doing any strenuous exercise, stretching your horse's muscles will enable him to perform better. Tight muscles produce a sore horse. Long and stretched muscles produce a relaxed horse.

This trotting exercise is an easy way to help you develop the lightest aids possible while you cultivate a feel for riding a horse with long, stretched muscles.

Schooling

1   Ask your horse to trot around the perimeter of the arena. Post the trot. Use your legs to tell him to move forward. Your hands lightly balance him so he doesn't pick up a canter. Hold yourself centered, relaxed, and balanced on the horse.

2   Pay attention to where the horse's impulsion comes from. If he is pulling himself along with his front legs, feel how slightly altering your balance or changing your hand position affects him. Practice until you can feel the horse using his hindquarters to push himself forward.

3   When the horse consistently pushes himself forward with his hind end, encourage him to stretch his body. Gently close your legs around his sides. Pay attention to how his neck feels as he trots. Ride him forward so that his neck starts to get *longer*, not *shorter*. Think: forward, out, and down.

4   Once the horse is stretching his head and neck forward while pushing from behind, feel the difference in his trot. Practice until you can have the horse push forward with his hind end and stretch forward with his head whenever you ask him to.

5   When your horse will consistently stretch his front end and push off with his hind end, pay attention to your weight. While the horse moves forward, concentrate on keeping your weight down in your heels. Feel how that anchors you to the horse.

6   Once your heels are well down, consciously pay attention to the position of your hands. Feel how light they can be while still being effective.

7   Trot on a circle, tracking to the right. When it feels good going to the right, change directions and track to the left. Periodically reevaluate how well your horse is moving, how well you can feel him, and how strong and correct your position is.

10.5 Focus on the horse's forward motion. Feel him push himself forward rather than pull himself along. The rider, however, neither pushes nor pulls, but rides in balance.

The Point

This exercise makes you aware of where the horse's impulsion comes from (fig. 10.5). You always want the horse to work from his hind legs and move forward from his hindquarters. The more you can get him working through his topline, the more comfortable and relaxed he will become. Moving forward correctly will also keep him sounder longer.

If you develop a feel for riding a horse lightly while he is working correctly, soon that will become the norm. Then you will always ride with that feeling as your goal.

● LOOKING AND SEEING

This simple exercise over fences is an excellent way to focus on riding with lightness and feeling the horse underneath you. It has the added benefit of developing your peripheral vision and honing an awareness of your surroundings.

Preparation

Set up a line of two low fences, 4 or 5 strides apart (for information on determining strides and distances, see "Relating Stride and Distance between Obstacles," p. 159). In the early stages, you may want to just use ground poles between jump standards.

Schooling

Find an object (such as a tree or a fence post) at the end of the line. Pick up a canter and focus your eyes on the object.

Continue to look at the object. As you allow the horse to navigate the line, pay attention to what you see with your peripheral vision (fig. 10.6). Notice everything—for instance:

- See your horse's head in front of you.
- See the oxer to your right that you don't want to run into.
- See the cone on the left that your horse might spook at.

- Be aware of traffic on the road nearby and take into consideration how that might affect your horse.

While your eyes are looking straight ahead and your peripheral vision is registering possible hazards, let your body feel what the horse is doing. Among other things:

- Feel how he reacts when he sees the fence in front of him.
- Feel how he responds when you close your legs on him.
- Feel the moment of suspension in each stride.
- Feel him tracking in a straight line toward the object you are looking at.
- Feel him accepting your hand and moving forward off of a light leg.

The Point

This exercise encourages you to be hyperaware of what happens as you ride a line. Remember, you only look straight ahead to where you are going. You also pay extra attention to your surroundings while you feel what is happening underneath you.

10.6 *As I ride the two-jump line, I raise my eyes and focus on a tree straight ahead. I can see all the potential distractions around me, including what remains of the tent, the open field, and the next jump.*

Coordinating Aids

Riding with lightness while maintaining an accurate feel for the horse requires effective coordination of aids. When you use the correct amount of seat, balance, hand, and leg together, your horse can understand what you are telling him to do. He can accept your instructions, relax, and respond to them.

Balancing Primary and Secondary Aids

Do not confuse "coordinating aids" with "equal aids." Coordinating your hands and legs does not mean that you must use equal amounts of pressure with both. Instead, it means that you need to balance the use of your hands and legs in order to get the desired result.

For any given movement, there are both primary and secondary aids available to help you accomplish your goals. Primary aids directly affect the horse's power and motion. Secondary aids restrict, redirect, or otherwise fine-tune the maneuver.

If, for instance, you want your horse to go forward, you will close your legs around him, use your spur, use your seat, or even use a cluck and a stick. These are your driving aids. They are your primary aids for impulsion.

The secondary aids are used to protect one aspect of the horse's performance while you ask him to do something else.

If you want your horse to travel in a straight line, the primary aids are your driving aids—whatever it takes to get him to carry you forward. The secondary aids in this situation are your rein aids. They do not directly affect the horse's impulsion. Instead, they ask him to stay straight as he moves ahead.

For another example, consider asking your horse to give with flexion. In this case, your hands on the reins are your primary aids. They apply pressure and ask the horse to accept it. When he does, he relaxes at his mouth, his poll, and his hind legs or his hocks. Yielding with flexion is his response to your primary aids.

While waiting for the horse to give with flexion, however, your legs are the secondary aids that ask him to continue working forward. They ensure that he does not go behind your leg and avoid responding to your hands.

Avoiding Conflict

When you apply the primary and secondary aids in a balanced, controlled way at the right time, your aids are coordinated. If you apply them at the wrong times, in the wrong order, or with the wrong amount of pressure, however, your aids are conflicting.

Essentially, conflicting aids tell the horse to do two different things at the same time (fig. 10.7). There is no way for him to accept the instructions or respond to them in a confident, relaxed manner.

An all-too-familiar example of conflicting aids is a rider who closes his legs and asks his horse to go forward while he has a death grip on the reins. His legs are saying, "Move!" but the hands say, "I won't let you." The horse can't do both.

10.7 *Conflicting aids create a confused or unhappy horse. More often than not, they also result in a sore or unsound horse.*

In order to avoid conflict and be able to coordinate your aids, you must develop an independent seat and independent hands (see "Aim for Independence," p. 132). Then you can more accurately control what aids influence the horse at any given time.

Exploring Jumping Releases

The *jumping release* allows your horse to stretch his head and neck out over a fence. It frees him up to use his body without hitting the bit while he is airborne.

In the earlier stages of learning, the jumping release also allows the rider to "hold on" without restricting the horse's motion.

Your jumping release will evolve over time. The more confident and competent you are as a rider, the more you will be able to maintain contact and influence the horse over a jump.

Long Release

The *long release* is the most basic release (fig. 10.8). It is appropriate for the rider who is just learning to jump.

For the long release, the rider moves both hands halfway up the crest of the horse's neck before the obstacle. He then pushes down on the crest to stabilize himself over the fence. He may also hold onto the horse's mane for added security.

10.8 *The long release loses contact with the horse through the entire jump. It gives the horse total freedom of his head and neck.*

Beginning riders may use the long release early, positioning the hands several strides before the jump and holding that position several strides after landing.

This release is best for beginners and intermediate riders because there is no danger of hurting the horse's mouth while he is jumping. It is used for two reasons. It completely turns the horse loose while the rider is learning so the rider doesn't interfere with the horse over the fence. It also helps the rider learn balance and support.

The one disadvantage to the long release is that it does not allow you to regulate your horse's rhythm, speed, or direction in the air. You must rely on the fact that you have directed the horse up to the approach. Then, when you let go for the long release, you must trust the horse to continue his pace, his stride, and his line.

Short Release

The *short release* involves the rider reaching about a quarter of the way up the horse's neck and pressing down with both hands. The reins are still loose, but are not thrown completely away as they are in the long release.

The short release is a less exaggerated, less obvious, less visible release. It doesn't happen quite as early before the jump, so the rider retains direction and control a bit longer.

The short release allows the intermediate rider to learn about feeling the horse's mouth a little bit off the ground. It enables the rider to somewhat influence the horse's speed and even shorten the jump, if necessary.

Automatic Release

The *automatic release* is for more advanced riders (fig. 10.9). In it, the rider's hands remain light and consistent on the horse's mouth throughout the jump. From the approach through the landing, the contact never changes.

When used correctly, the automatic release allows the horse to use his neck in exactly the same way as a long release that gave him total freedom.

With the automatic release, you can continue to direct the horse even in the air. The drawback is, if you do not have independent hands and an independent seat, you might inhibit the jump or create stiffness that would cause the horse to drop his hind end and hit the jump or knock down a rail.

When you ride with contact, your hands are able to regulate every step your horse takes (fig. 10.10). Contact allows you to maintain the horse's stride, and shorten or lengthen it. The automatic release enables you to regulate the horse's "flight stride": in other words, as the horse leaves the ground for the jump, the automatic release lets you think of that jump as just another stride.

10.9 *The automatic release retains contact over the jump but allows the horse to use his neck as much as he wants.*

10.10 *The automatic release may be used to shorten the horse's neck, shorten his jump, and shorten his landing.*

● LEARNING THE AUTOMATIC RELEASE

When you are ready for the automatic release, one of the best ways to learn it is to turn your hands around on the reins.

Instead of having the reins come from the horse's mouth up through the bottom of your hands, with the excess running out between your thumb

10.11 *Learn the automatic release with the reins running from the bit to the top of your forefinger. Let the "bight" of the reins go between your thumb and forefinger, down through your hand, and out by your little finger.*

and forefinger, practice with the reins running from the bit *down* through your thumb and forefinger to come out at the bottom of your hands by your little finger (fig. 10.11).

My students find that changing the hand position in this way is most effective in teaching the rider how to follow the horse's mouth, head, and neck through the arc of the jump.

Anatomy of a Jump

From the lowest cross-rail to Grand Prix stadium jumps, every fence on every course involves the same basic elements. How well you perform each individual element determines how successful, correct, and smooth your overall jump will be.

Approach

The ideal approach is a straight line. The line may run through the center of the jump. It may fall to one side or the other of the center. It may angle across the jump. It may even follow a curve. (In this case, "a straight line on a curve" is not an oxymoron. It simply means following a clearly planned, consistent path without cutting in or bulging out.)

Throughout the entire approach, your job as the rider is to continue on a specific straight line at an even pace (fig. 10.13). Set the pace that you think the jump—and the line after it—requires.

Once you have set your pace, keep it consistent while you wait for distance. On the approach, maintaining your line and pace will show you the distance, which is the takeoff.

Takeoff

The correct distance for your takeoff is where you arrive at the jump and can take off relaxed, without pushing or pulling (fig. 10.14). The perfect distance is not a particular spot on the ground. It's a feeling of arriving at the jump so that you don't have to *do* anything to get over it.

JUDGE'S CARD
BEWARE OF EXAGGERATION

Some people do not understand the correct use of the automatic release and are opposed to using it. In fact, they will often exaggerate the long release—throwing their hands and body forward and making a big deal of *not* using the automatic release.

These people, through their theatrics, draw attention to their hands, their body position, and their horse's effort over the fence. More often than not, their expansive movements actually work against the horse's natural motion in the air and can interfere with his jump.

10.12 *What not to do: the incorrect "low release." Breaking the line from the elbow to the bit below the mouth interrupts the forward flow of the jump. The horse's expression reflects his opinion of the release.*

As a judge, if I see a rider using an exaggerated long release, throwing his hands around, dropping contact early, and not taking it up on the landing side, I will fault such distracting, sloppy riding.

Other riders exaggerate the automatic release and turn it into something they call the "low release." In the low release, the rider throws his hands down, emphasizing that he is maintaining contact without going up on the horse's neck (fig. 10.12).

These people, through their exaggeration, go below the line of the horse's mouth with their contact and often interfere with the horse's jump. Using a release that is heavy and breaks below the line of the mouth will cause the horse to jump with his head up and make it difficult for him to follow through behind.

When judging, if I see a rider who is not releasing, or stiffing the horse, or working below the line with the automatic release, that has a direct bearing either on his riding (for Hunt Seat Equitation classes) or his horse's round (in Hunter divisions). More likely than not, such a rider has a horse that jumps with his head high, doesn't follow through, or has unnecessary rubs or knocks rails down behind, and I will fault that.

What I look for as a judge is an action that I don't notice. It doesn't matter which release you use. I shouldn't notice it because you don't draw unnecessary attention to your hands, your position doesn't change, and your horse jumps with beautiful style and expression.

10.13 *The approach: find your line, establish your pace, and keep both absolutely consistent.*

10.14 *The ideal takeoff allows the horse to take the jump in stride, without pushing or pulling on the rider's part.*

The Jump

The perfect jump is fluid, symmetrical, and relaxed (fig. 10.15). It falls in the same rhythm as the pace leading up to it. It continues along the original "flight plan," and follows the line of the approach.

Landing

The line you use in your approach is the line you hold across the jump. It is also the line you continue to follow when you land. Unless you are doing something specific in order to make the next fence, you should land at the same pace as your approach, takeoff, and jump (fig. 10.16).

Departure

As you move away from the jump and head toward the next obstacle, you should maintain the same line, at the same pace, and your horse should still be relaxed.

Relating Stride and Distance between Obstacles

The key to understanding distance is understanding how your horse's stride relates to the jump course. At a regular canter or hand gallop, an average horse covers 12 feet in a single stride. Therefore, most courses, lines, and distances are based on the premise that the horse is working with a 12-foot stride.

10.15 *The jump should be symmetrical, with the horse's body tracing a beautiful, round arc over the obstacle.*

10.16 *The landing is the best way to "grade" your jump. If the landing is relaxed, you have had a good jump.*

Distances between fences take takeoffs and landings into account. The normal takeoff for a jump is 6 feet, and 6 feet is also allotted for the normal landing from a jump.

Determining your horse's stride, then, is based on these measurements:

- 12-foot stride
- 6-foot takeoff
- 6-foot landing

The "Home Base" Pace

Generally speaking, the faster the horse's speed, the longer his stride. The key to determining when your horse is taking 12-foot strides is to ride him at varying speeds over a line set for a 12-foot stride.

Every time you ride the line, keep the pace absolutely consistent from one fence to the other until you find the right speed that allows the horse to take each jump perfectly. Once you have found it, that speed becomes your horse's *home base pace.*

Knowing your horse's home base pace is invaluable on the jump course. Armed with that knowledge, you should be able to walk any new course (more on that in "Walking a Course," p. 167) and identify the following:

- Normal Lines   Lines of fences set up for a 12-foot stride.
- Steady (or Slow) Lines   Lines of jumps set up for a slightly *shorter* stride than normal and requiring a slightly *slower* pace (figs. 10.17 A & B).
- Forward Lines   Lines of jumps set up for a slightly *longer* stride than normal and requiring a slightly *faster* pace (figs. 10.17 C & D).

● FINDING "HOME BASE"

One of the best ways to find your horse's home base pace is to use the 5-stride line. It gives you enough room to feel the speed and remember it, but not so much room that you have too many variables to deal with.

Preparation

Plan for 5 strides that are each 12 feet long (5 x 12 = 60). Then, remember to include a 6-foot landing coming off the first jump, and a 6-foot takeoff before

10.17 A *Landing and departure in a steady or slow line. Use light contact to ask the horse to land as close to the jump as possible.*

B *Bring the horse's balance up and ask him to continue shortening his stride away from the jump.*

C *Landing and departure in a very forward line. Allow the horse to stretch as long as he can. Ask him to land as far from the jump as possible.*

D *After landing, continue stretching the horse's stride. Compare the rider's angles and the horse's length of stride in both the slow line and the forward line.*

the last jump (60 + 6 + 6 = 72). (See "The Home Practice Course," fig. 11.6, p. 178, for a suggested set-up, and also see "Using a Line," p. 164, and "Eyeing the Line," p. 189, for more practice with the 5-stride line.)

Set up one fence and—72 feet away, in a perfectly straight line—set up another. The fences don't have to be high to be effective. Keeping the fences low will allow you to concentrate more on the horse's pace than on getting over the jump.

Schooling

Canter the line. As you approach the first fence, establish the horse's pace and maintain that pace through to the second fence.

Canter the line back and forth. Experiment with different speeds until you find the one that allows your horse to canter or gallop the line in both directions in 5 even strides.

The Point

When you find the pace that allows you to easily take both fences with 5 even, consistent strides between them, you are working on a 12-foot stride. Work at that speed until you are completely familiar with it. *That* is your home base pace.

Counting Strides

Knowing the number of strides between fences is a huge help. It makes for more comfortable decision making. It makes the rider's job a little easier.

Unfortunately, too many riders have allowed counting strides to become a crutch. In reality, riding a line correctly depends far more on knowing what pace the line requires than on knowing the number of strides to get from one fence to the next.

In other words, if someone says to you, "That's a 5-stride line," you don't have enough information to ride the line as well as possible. You must assume it is a normal 5 strides (72 feet) and ride it at your horse's home base pace. You have to jump into the line, land at that pace, and then rely on your timing and experience to let you know if you should speed up or slow down.

Let's assume that the line is slightly longer than 72 feet. Unless you know ahead of time that it is a "forward line," you won't work with more pace as you approach the first jump. More than likely, you will be in the middle of the line before you realize that the distance to the second fence is longer than normal. Then it is too late to increase your pace so the line rides evenly.

On the other hand, let's say that the line is slightly less than 72 feet. If you have no idea how many strides it is, but know the line is a steady one, to be ridden quietly or slowly, you are more likely to ride it correctly than if you approach it armed only with the knowledge that it should take 5 strides to get from the first fence to the second.

10.18 *"Distance"—finding the perfect takeoff point—is the element most difficult for the rider to control.*

Understanding the Factors of Jumping

Four factors make up every successful jump: pace, line, balance, and distance.

In order to be comfortable with distance, you must control the other three factors as much as possible and amass a repertoire of tools to bring you in at the correct place at the right time.

Exercises to Develop a Feel for Distance

● USING A LINE

Once you know your horse's pace for a 12-foot stride (see "Finding 'Home Base'" on p. 160), working at that pace over a familiar line can help develop your feel for distance.

Preparation

Use the same 5-stride line of two fences set 72 feet apart that you used for "Finding 'Home Base.'"

Schooling

1 Approach the line in what you think would be your normal pace. Look at the highest point of the jump as you approach it. Don't try to find a specific spot on the ground. Just feel your horse and make sure he is working at the pace you want.

2 Never drop your eyes. As your horse nears the first fence and you sense he is getting ready to take it, raise your eyes and look at the highest point of the second jump.

3 Jump the first fence and continue toward the second. The object is to arrive at the second jump in such a way that you can relax on stride five, and your horse will give you a nice jump (fig. 10.19).

If you are pulling on stride five, your distance is too deep. If you are "gassing" your horse, or using a strong leg and seat, you have arrived too late and your distance is too long.

10.19 When you arrive where you can relax, using no hands to slow the horse and no legs to urge him faster, you have hit the distance to the second fence just right.

The Point

Once you know your horse's normal pace, concentrated work on a 5-stride line will teach you how to fine-tune his speed or regulate his stride. The goal is always to jump an obstacle so that both horse and rider are as relaxed as possible.

● ONE JUMP ON A CIRCLE

This is an excellent exercise to improve your feel for distance. Practice it at the walk and the trot first. Then do it at the canter. Regardless of the pace you choose, the speed stays even both on the circle and over the jump.

Preparation

Set up a single, simple vertical that can be jumped from both directions. Keep the jump low—a simple ground pole will do—so you do not worry about clearing it and can focus on the exercise. The area around the fence should be free of clutter and other obstacles (fig. 10.20).

Schooling

1 Establish a consistent pace and circle.

2 Focus on the highest part of the center of the jump during your approach. As you near the obstacle, keep your eye ahead of you on the path you want the horse to follow.

3 Concentrate on the circle, not on the fence. Consciously feel the circle. Make certain that it never changes. Your horse should not cut in or bulge out.

4 Remember, circle size is related to your speed. If you are doing a posting trot, the circle can be fairly small. At the canter, the circle must be a little larger. If you want to practice at a real galloping pace, you will have to work on a very large circle.

5 For the better part of the circle, your pace and your line should stay the same with every stride. Then, when you look ahead to the jump, you will start to get a sense of whether you need to slow down a bit to avoid hitting the rail or whether you should speed up a bit in order to make the rail.

The Point

Make slight adjustments to be sure the distance to the jump will work so that on the last stride you can relax. In other words, if you are getting there late, you want a slight overall increase in stride so that on the last stride you can relax. If you are getting there deep, you want to slow down a little bit so that you can relax for the jump itself.

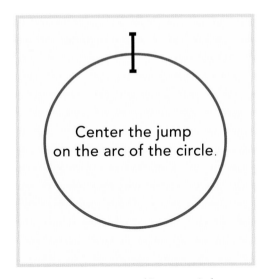

Center the jump on the arc of the circle.

10.20 *Concentrate on making your circle absolutely round and keeping your pace.*

The "50 Percent" Rule

When considering distance, regardless of whether you are jumping a straight line, an angled jump, or a jump on a circle, if you keep your pace and line exactly the same from approach through departure, the *worst* you can do is meet that jump half a stride wrong.

If you really mess up your distance or timing, your horse might meet the fence half a stride too long or half a stride too short. Any horse that is worth anything can make up half a stride. That is why it becomes critical not to change your pace or change your line.

If, however, you concentrate on distance, your line and your pace will vary. If you change either your line or your pace on the approach to the jump, instead of finding your distance, you will be avoiding it. You will either speed up, or slow down, or move off your line. All these errors will give you a false read on the jump.

Your best bet is to keep your eye on the highest point of the jump. Feel that your horse's stride stays the same. Feel that your line stays the same. A consistent stride and an unwavering line will give you your distance.

Sweet Simplicity

Simplicity is the best. Not only are the previous two exercises an excellent way to help develop a feel for distance (a much more accurate term than an "eye for distance"), but they are useful for fine-tuning your pace and timing as well.

If I am at the Medal Finals, and a student starts taking things too seriously—if his nerves are getting in the way of his riding, if he has had too much thrown at him, or if the course is so complicated that it seems overwhelming—these exercises are lifesavers.

Often in such situations, I will set up a 5-stride line and have the student simply jump it back and forth until he gets comfortable again with the right pace. If the student's timing is a little off, I might put up just one fence and have him jump it in a circle from both directions until he gets it.

You will never be such a good rider that you have no need for the basics. Every once in awhile, if all the factors of riding seem to be getting more and more complex, revisit what you already know. Going back to the simplest exercises will help you develop confidence and find your feel again.

Walking a Course

Whenever possible before jumping a course, go over it on foot. Walk the distance between jumps (fig. 10.21). Walk the turns. Look at the types of jumps. Check the footing. See if the cups are deep or shallow. Walking a course can give you an invaluable understanding of the jumps you will face before you are actually in the ring riding over them.

To make the most of walking the course, allow enough time to gather the information you need. As you walk, prioritize what you learn. I believe walking a course is critical if you want to be competitive.

How to Walk a Distance

At home, lay a yardstick on the ground and practice making one of your strides equal 3 feet. If you walk with a 3-foot stride, and your horse travels on a 12-foot stride, then every four steps of yours will add up to one of his strides.

Then, mark off a distance of 36 or 42 feet and practice walking it. Practice until you are consistently accurate in your measurement.

Count to yourself in sets of four: "**1**-2-3-4, **2**-2-3-4, **3**-2-3-4…" Count until you reach the next jump.

What You Can Learn

Let's say your counting takes you up to "**6**-2-3-4" and stops exactly at the second jump in the line. Take away one set of four steps (6 feet for the landing on jump one and 6 feet for the takeoff on jump two). You are left with 5, 12-foot strides between those two jumps, which means it is a normal 5-stride line.

The reason to walk from jump to jump is because you will want to know if a line is normal, steady (short), or forward (long).

If the line doesn't work out perfectly so that you have an even division of 12 feet between fences, the number of steps you take after each count of "4" determines whether you add a stride or take one out.

10.21 When walking a course, walk the whole distance from one jump to the other. Do not walk from the estimated landing of one fence to the estimated takeoff of another. Stand with your back right against the jump and pace off 3-foot strides between it and the next jump.

- *One* extra step means it is a long line and should be ridden at a more forward pace.
- *Two* extra steps mean you have to decide whether to shorten the horse's stride and add a stride, or lengthen the horse's stride and try to do the line in a very forward manner.
- *Three* extra steps almost always mean that you should go with the shorter option for that line.

If you count only **6-2-3**, you will know that the line is slightly shorter than normal. Five shorter, steady strides are needed to make the second fence work.

If you count to **6-2-3-4**, and have another step ahead of you, then you know it is a long 5-stride line. You will have to ride it with more pace in order to keep the strides even and jump the fence smoothly.

If you count **6-2-3-4**, and have two steps ahead of you, then you know that is a 5½-stride line. That means you have the option of extending your horse's stride and riding him more forward to do the line in 5 strides. You could also collect your horse, shorten his stride a bit, and do the line in 6 strides.

Use the jumps and their direction on the course to determine which option you will choose. In this situation, if you have two verticals heading away from home, a steady 6 strides is probably called for. If you have two oxers toward home, a forward 5 is probably your best bet.

If you end up counting **6-2-3-4, 7-2-3**, then you know you will have to ride the line in a steady, slow, six strides instead of a forward five.

Walking with Purpose

Often, when people walk courses, they just walk the numbers. While it is certainly important to know the numbers, or the strides, between the jumps, it is also important to understand the type of jump, and what will be asked of the horse after the jump.

For example, a normal 5-stride line to a spooky jump becomes a forward 5 strides to compensate for the potential spook. Jumping toward the side of the arena will ride differently than having nothing but an open space after the fence. And you will want to ride toward home more softly than away from home. Taking all the variables into consideration will help you achieve a more even, consistent course.

When walking a course, analyze the following for each obstacle:

- **Jump Type**   Is it a vertical or is it an oxer? How tall is it? How wide?
- **Location**   Where will the horse be galloping as he heads to the jump? Is it toward or away from home? Are there any potential distractions to one side or the other?
- **Relationship to Others**   If the jump is part of a line, how does the line ride? Is the distance slow, forward, or just right? What are the other jumps in the line?
- **Takeoffs**   What are the approaches like? Are they long or short? How is the footing?
- **Landings**   Do you have to land on the same line, land on a different straight line, or land on a curve to the next jump? What is the footing like on the departures?
- **Construction**   Are there clear ground lines? Are the jump cups deep or flat? How solidly in place is the top rail? The more "careful" a jump, the more accurate you need to be as you ride it.

Typecasting for Success

Before jumping an unfamiliar course, it can be very helpful to "type" your horse and yourself in relation to the various obstacles you will encounter. Make certain you see the problem spots on the course ahead of time. Identify what will be most challenging to you and plan a way to tackle it.

For example, if you are an anxious or timid rider, you will want to be boldest on forward lines, spooky lines, unusual jumps, or long approaches—whatever makes you nervous.

If you are a rider that goes faster when you get nervous, the short, steady lines on the course will require extra attention.

Typing your horse is even more important. Try to describe your horse according to what influences him the most. Ask yourself: If I were riding my horse for the first time over this new course, what one thing would I most need to know? Is the horse short-strided? Long-strided? Spooky? Careful?

Pick a quality that best characterizes the horse, then apply that to the course and see where the challenges arise.

When you are done "typecasting," you should be able to review the course in very concise terms. You should know what areas will challenge you and what areas will challenge your horse.

You won't be able to do it all. Avoid the temptation to microanalyze every aspect of your position over every fence. Rather, walk the course, look at all the factors and prioritize them. Decide which are the most important things and focus on them. Then rely on your habits, your knowledge, and your experience to take care of the rest.

Memorizing Courses

Many riders have difficulty when it comes to memorizing courses. Often, the biggest fear of a competitor on show day is forgetting the course in the middle of the ring. Some suggestions for mastering memorization:

- Memorizing your course is generally easiest if you begin with the *course chart*. The chart gives you a visual representation of the whole layout. Looking at the course on paper helps you see the pattern of it and gives you a sense of things in general.

- It may help to think in terms of *lines*, rather than trying to memorize arbitrary fence numbers. Break the course down into pieces (outside line, diagonal line, end jump, combination). Then put the pieces together to form a logical pattern.

- Identifying a jump by a *characteristic* ("the skinny one," "the end jump," "the coop") is often more useful than referring to it by number.

- Pay attention to *leads* and where *home* is. You might think, "The first line is left lead away… the second line is left lead home… the last one is right lead away…" It can bring your course into focus in an easily remembered, manageable way.

- Sometimes you may have to do back-to-back rounds of different courses without leaving the ring between rounds. Often, however, the *first jump* will dictate the rest of the course. In hunter classes, for instance, if you know the first jump, there is usually only one way the pattern can work. So, if you are doing back-to-back trips, you can easily remember two courses just by remembering the first jump for each.

- *Color* can also help with your memorizing. Jumps in a line are often the same color. You could think, "The red line, to the blue line, to the yellow line, to the blue line." Red—blue—yellow—blue could describe your whole course.
- *Visualizing* is very helpful. Think in terms of patterns and shapes. When necessary, break the course down into pieces. Memorize the course chart. Then look at the course while looking at the chart. Make sure you understand the corresponding jumps. (Sometimes the course in the ring doesn't always look the same as it did on paper and it can be confusing.) Then look away from the course. Close your eyes and make sure you know the course in your head. Be able to "see" the course without the chart and without the jumps in front of you.

11

Course Work

Be Prepared

A jumping course is composed of a series of tests. Riders are judged on their proficiency at jumping fences in straight lines and on curves. They may be asked to change directions, to change the horse's speed, or to alter his stride. They may be required to jump some fences straight-on and jump others at angles.

Even the most difficult course is nothing more than the sum of its parts. To do well, you must be able to first identify —and then master—the parts.

In other words, don't just go out and endlessly jump courses. Instead, spend your practice time on exercises that will give you the skills you need. Then, when the time comes, you will be able to apply what you have learned to any course you encounter.

Rails on the Ground

Working over ground-rails is one of the best-kept secrets for learning a feel for distance (fig. 11.2). A horse going to a jump will help gauge and measure distance for you. On the way to a rail, the horse is less apt to do that. So riding over ground-rails (as opposed to over

11.1 *Though every course is different, the abilities tested remain the same.*

11.2 *Ground-rails are very effective for teaching pace and line.*

actual jumps) can help you develop a more precise ride and a better feel.

Furthermore, ground-rails allow you to repeat an exercise until you get it, without as much wear and tear on your horse.

Fence Construction

Fences may or may not include *ground lines*. A ground line is a pole, rail, or other solid object across the bottom of the fence to give the horse a clear indication of the jump's base. It is more difficult to accurately judge the distance to fences without ground lines.

Whenever possible, set up your practice fences so you can jump them from both directions. If using ground lines, this means to include one on both sides of the fence. It also means using square oxers (with both elements the same height), as opposed to ramped ones (with one element higher than the other).

Furthermore, in order to safely jump a fence from any direction, it must be able to "break away" to either side. If the horse hits the fence as he goes over it, the middle of the fence—whether it is made up of rails, brush, or boxes—must fall cleanly.

Practical Considerations

If in doubt, always set a jump too low rather than too high. Make your practice oxers too narrow rather than too wide. You want to focus on your job and concentrate on what you are learning rather than being distracted by the fear that the jump is too high.

Bear in mind, however, that bigger, higher fences are more difficult than smaller, lower ones. Every so often, find the time to fit a few larger obstacles into your practice rides. You need to be comfortable jumping fences at the height (or even a little higher) that you will be expected to clear in competition.

Learn low (fig. 11.3). But, be able to do slightly more at home than you will have to do in the show ring. For example, let's say that you will be competing in a division with 3' 6" fences. It would make sense to set your home course at 3' 6", with a fence or two at 3' 9".

During practice, while you are mastering different elements of the course, you could make the verticals into cross-rails or take out elements in order to lower the jumps. That way, you can learn things like line, pace, and better position at a lower height. Then you can easily put the rails up into the cups and repeat the ride over the higher fences.

Types of Jumps

Every show you attend will have fences that are different than yours at home. Including many different kinds of jumps in your practice is an important part of your foundation.

Some basic fence constructions that you should be familiar with include:

- **Cross-rails** These are some of the simplest fences. They are made of two rails—each with one end resting in a jump cup and with the other end angled down to the ground—crossed to form an "X." In a cross-rail, the center of the jump is always the lowest part (fig. 11.4).
- **Verticals** The vertical fence has no spread to it. The higher the vertical, the more the horse's jump follows a steep arc. A vertical can be an airy single rail across two standards, or it can be more elaborate, with more "fill" between the top rail and the ground.

11.3 *Set fences low for learning.*

11.4 *Cross-rails are invaluable for riders learning to jump. They are also effective for teaching the rider to jump over the fence's center.*

11.5 Crossing the rails of an oxer into a modified Swedish oxer will make the jump lower and easier to practice. Place the ends of the rails on the ground to the inside, rather than the outside, of the standards to ensure that the fence falls in the right direction if the horse hits it.

- **Skinny Jumps**   The normal width of a jump is 12 feet. A jump may be as narrow as 6 or 9 feet, however. Practice jumping obstacles that are narrower than normal so your horse gets more comfortable navigating the tighter space.
- **Walls**   These are solidly constructed fences. The bottom of the wall usually rests on the ground, with rails placed over the wall to make the jump higher.
- **Oxers**   An oxer is considered a single obstacle. It is made of two sets of standards placed closely enough together that the rails from both are jumped at the same time. Oxers come in several varieties including parallel or square (both front and back rails are at the same height), ramp, and Swedish (both front and back sets of standards have the same number of rails to them, with the rails of the front element higher on one side, and the rails of the back element higher on the other—fig. 11.5).
- **Triple Bars**   Similar to oxers, triple bars are three sets of standards with their rails placed closely together so the horse clears them all in a single jump. Triple bars challenge the horse's ability to jump both high and wide.
- **Combinations**   While combinations are considered a type of fence, it would be more accurate to describe them as a type of line. These series test the horse's ability to clear fence after fence with no strides (bounce), 1 stride, or 2 strides between fences. Two-fence combinations are called *in-and-outs*. Combinations are excellent gymnastic exercises for you and your horse.

• Scary Jumps   This category includes every kind of jump your horse has never seen before that causes him to spook in the show ring. While you can't always simulate the exact obstacles you will have to navigate, you *can* get your horse used to jumping a variety of different fences.

Have fun. Be creative when constructing your jumps. Go through the barn and collect "fence fill": drape coolers or blankets over rails; use wheelbarrows as oxer fill; use lawn chairs as standards; fill buckets with water and set them as a ground line; use tree branches or potted plants for brushy fill. Don't just jump the same old boring rails. Create different experiences for you and your horse.

When Your Number Is Up

A horse is not a machine. Every takeoff, every landing, every rollback, and every turn takes its toll on his body.

In a very real sense, each horse has a finite number of good jumps in his lifetime. You have to always, *always* be aware of how many jumps you are using up.

In other words, if your horse has one million jumps in him, every fence you take means one less fence you can jump later. Therefore, it is critical that you use those jumps wisely. Make each one count.

The Home Course Advantage

Since every course consists of a series of tests, it is in your best interest to practice at home what you will encounter in competition. The ideal home course should include examples of the tests you can expect to find at a show.

You will rarely know your course pattern before the event. That is why you must become proficient at all of the pieces you may be tested over. Then, when show day arrives and you see how the course is constructed, you can draw on the skills you have amassed and use them to help you put together the perfect round.

Preparing the Practice Course

The remainder of this chapter examines the various elements of typical courses. In order to do so, it uses an easy-to-set-up practice course that incorporates each element in its design (fig. 11.6).

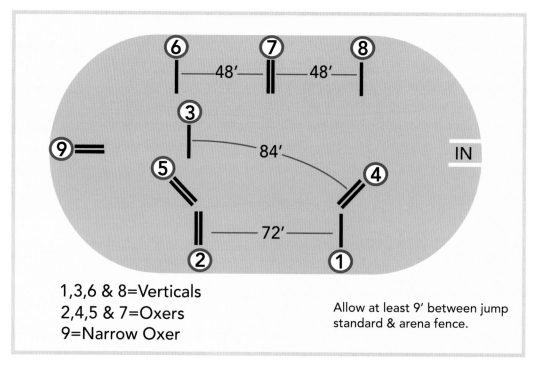

1,3,6 & 8=Verticals
2,4,5 & 7=Oxers
9=Narrow Oxer

Allow at least 9' between jump standard & arena fence.

11.6 *The "Home Practice" Course.*

When building your own practice course, pay special attention to the distances between fences. Pace off the distances to get a feel for walking a course. Then, be sure to measure the distances, so you know they are exact.

Set up your fences so they may be jumped from both directions (see "Fence Construction," p. 174). Be careful to set your practice fences low to begin with. You can always raise them later on, once you have an understanding of each exercise.

COURTESY CIRCLES

Every course begins and ends with a courtesy circle. The circle begins at a walk or a trot and then progresses into a canter or gallop. It is usually no more than 20 meters in diameter.

Don't Cross the Dotted Line

In major horse shows with many horses and many classes, management often uses a "dotted line" on the course to keep the circles small. Small circles mean the riders start jumping their courses soon after entering the ring. This keeps things moving and gets the day done faster.

The dotted line is an imaginary boundary marked on the course chart. The actual course may also have bushes or little pieces of rail strategically placed to signify where the dotted line falls.

In a show, passing the dotted line on either your courtesy circle or your closing circle will eliminate you from the round. Therefore, the first thing you need to determine when planning your circle is whether or not the course has a dotted line.

Know Your Horse

The better you know your horse, the more you can use the courtesy circle to your advantage. If you are smart, you can use the circle to show the horse the course or to show him off to the judge. For example:

- If your horse is cold and needs to get geared up for the course, make your opening circle as large possible. March right into the ring at the trot. To engage your horse's brain a bit, bring him back to an animated walk. Then send him into the canter. If there is no dotted line, make a big circle right through the middle of the ring. That gives you time to get up to pace with your horse alert and responding well.
- If you have a hot horse, walk into the ring and spend much of your courtesy circle letting him just get settled into the environment. Then, at the last minute, softly pick up a gallop and head to your first fence.
- If you have a horse that is spooky about the jumps, you might do best with

COURTESY CIRCLES

11.7 *Bend the horse's head away from a jump he may spook at. Use an indirect rein and your leg to move his body toward the jump while riding your courtesy circle.*

a maze-like sort of courtesy circle. Ride past the spookiest jumps in the ring to get the horse comfortable seeing them before you ask him to jump them (fig. 11.7).

• If you have a horse that is a bad mover, but a great jumper, don't spend a lot of time on the courtesy circle. Walk into the ring, pick up a canter, and get right to the jumping part, which is your horse's forte.

• If, on the other hand, you have a horse that moves beautifully at the trot, it is in your best interest to trot a huge portion of the courtesy circle. If you have a horse that has a beautiful gallop, the same principle applies: walk in and pick up your canter almost immediately. Then use the circle to showcase your horse's spectacular gait in front of the judge.

The Closing Circle

The closing circle is a way of "closing the book" on the course. It shows a deliberate end to your ride. It also gives you a final opportunity to impress the judge with your precision and your horse's brilliance.

Whenever possible, make a big closing circle through the middle of the ring. Get your horse in the habit of going past the first line of jumps and away from the in-gate before he heads out of the ring.

If you have a dotted line for the opening and closing circles, of course, your options are limited. (I personally think the dotted line for a closing circle is a bad thing. It teaches you to finish your last jump, spin in a small circle, and then ride out the gate. I do not advise practicing that at home.)

Regardless of the closing circle's dimensions, keep your pace. It is good practice to stay at a steady, consistent gallop after your last fence. Wait to bring your horse back to a trot or walk until you are headed toward the gate.

● COURTESY BEGINS AT HOME

Preparation

Once you understand courtesy circles, there is rarely a need to practice them when you are at home. It is a good idea, however, to familiarize yourself with them, and to be comfortable riding them on courses with and without dotted lines.

Since the courtesy circle is different for every course, there is no need to rearrange your home course in order to practice.

Schooling

When familiarizing yourself with courtesy circles, ride several practice circles of different diameters. Determine in advance where the "judge" will be and what your first fence is.

Begin some circles at a walk. Begin others at a trot. Practice picking up your canter or gallop at different stages of the circle and see how that affects your horse's ability to get up to his working pace.

Become comfortable with executing the courtesy circle in varying situations. Imagine that the "judge" is in a different location, or that your first fence has changed.

As an interesting exercise, systematically consider each fence in the ring and determine an appropriate courtesy circle for that fence should it be the first in a course.

The Point

Courtesy circles are like "bookends" for your course. Your opening circle brings you up to pace before you ride to the first jump. At the end of a course, a closing circle allows you to finish the ride in a controlled, deliberate manner, rather than simply rushing out the exit gate after your last fence.

The courtesy circle is more than just an easy ride on the flat as you approach your first obstacle. It is your first opportunity to make a good impression on the judge. It is also your last chance to school your horse before starting the course. Understanding your horse's strengths and weaknesses can help you use the courtesy circle to your advantage.

COURTESY CIRCLES

11.8 *Don't let a wrong lead wreck your concentration. Catch it as quickly as possible, correct it, and continue.*

What Can Go Wrong & How to Fix It

- **Loss of Forward Motion**   Forward motion is difficult to establish if your horse is feeling cramped. Be sure to give your horse enough room to work forward while you are beginning, or finishing, your course.

- **Stopping, Spooking, or Balking**   If your horse is a bit uncertain, don't start your circle heading right toward something that might bother him. If you do, he might spin around, stop, spook sideways, or rear. Each response is equal to a refusal in front of a fence, and the judges would score it accordingly. At the show you must carefully plan how you will approach spooky fences. Find a way to get into the ring so you are not immediately facing any problem areas. If possible, let your horse see the fences at an angle first, before meeting them straight on. At home, add greenery, flapping flags or buckets of water to get your horse used to seeing "scary" things.

- **Picking Up the Wrong Lead**   In equitation classes, judges see this as a serious mistake. In the Hunter and Jumper divisions, it's not as serious. If you pick up the wrong lead, you should make a flying change to the correct lead. (The theory is, if you come back to the walk or the trot to fix a canter on the wrong lead, you have made a break of gait, or a loss of forward motion.) If you do pick up the wrong lead, however, realize that the judges are interested in the best jumper (fig. 11.8).

- **Crossing the Dotted Line**   As discussed earlier, this results in elimination from the round. Carefully map out a planned route ahead of time, taking all boundaries into consideration.

- **Jigging**   If you plan to walk part of your courtesy circle, but your horse is so excited that he is jigging, just put him into the canter and get to work. Give him a job to do, rather than try to force him to stay quiet.

SINGLE JUMPS

In a lot of ways, single fences are the easiest to jump. They stand alone—literally. You can analyze your approach and departure for a single fence without having to take into account other jumps just before or just after it.

The Single Scene

Identifying the single jump on a course is not difficult: it is the fence that doesn't fall in line with any other.

In the hunter world, courses often begin with a single jump. Single jumps generally have a long approach on a diagonal or an outside line (figs. 11.9 A & B).

The long approach tends to cause more concern than the jump itself. For some reason, many riders worry about a jump that is by itself out in the open, particularly if they have a lot of time on their approach.

Single on a Circle

A great exercise for learning to jump single fences is riding one jump on a circle (see p. 165). It will enhance your feel for distance and make you more comfortable riding a longer approach.

On your practice course, Fence 1 lends itself to being ridden on a circle because of the wide open space around it. Depending on the size of your arena, other fences in the practice course may also be used for this exercise.

Establish your pace and your circle. Then ride Fence 1 at the trot and the canter from both directions until you are comfortable going over it.

11.9 A *Establish your home base pace on the approach to the single fence. Do not change your pace or your line.*

B *When you see your distance to the fence, relax and let the horse do his job.*

SINGLE JUMPS

Another exercise for practicing single fences involves an imaginary line:

● THE IMAGINARY LINE

Preparation

In your practice course, both Fence 3 and Fence 5 are ideal for this exercise. Remember to keep the fences low at first.

Walk off a distance of 72 feet from the fence you will be jumping. Place buckets or cones on either side of an imaginary ground pole as mini jump standards to mark the distance.

Schooling

1 Establish your pace for a normal 5-stride line.
2 Ride straight through the imaginary jump. Maintain your pace and your line. Treat the real jump as if it is the second fence in the line (figs. 11.10 A & B).
3 Ride the imaginary line from both directions. Get comfortable jumping the single fence as either the first or the second "obstacle" in the line.
4 When you are consistently keeping your pace even and your line straight, remove the markers and ride the fence from both directions.

The Point

Use your familiarity with the 5-stride line to help you maintain a consistent pace and line to the fence. Riding the fence as if it is the first in a 5-stride line prepares you for single fences with shorter approaches. Riding it as if it is the second fence of a line gives you a feel for a longer approach.

What Can Go Wrong & How to Fix It

• **Speeding Up When Going One Direction**   Some horses will try to rush over the jump if they are headed toward home. If your horse insists on speeding up toward home, practice jumping one jump on a circle for a while (see p. 165). Ride the circle so the jump is toward home. Work on establishing an absolutely consistent, even pace. Then, go back and work on your imaginary line.

11.10 A *Treat the imaginary fence as if it is the first in the line.*

B *Keep your pace absolutely consistent as you ride toward the real fence. Take the fence in stride.*

SINGLE JUMPS

- **You Get Nervous on the Long Approach**   Try not to concentrate on your nerves. Instead, work on keeping your pace exactly even and consistent. Focus on controlling your pace until you feel the jump is going to work.
- **Veering Off the Line**   It is sometimes difficult, especially on the diagonal (as with Fence 5), to stay on your chosen line. Fix your eyes to the highest point of your jump as you approach it. Don't let your eyes drop, even for a second. Use them to "reel you in" on a straight, unswerving approach.
- **Losing Pace**   On long approaches to single oxers (as with Fence 5), the hardest thing to do is make yourself stay up to pace. It is tempting to slow down until you see your distance. Unfortunately, slowing down arrests the horse's forward motion and puts him in a backward mode. Make yourself keep your horse up to pace. Feel that he is in front of your legs and relaxed at that pace. Then, look to your jump. Remember, you don't adjust your pace to find the distance; you find the distance and then adjust your pace.
- **Landing on the Wrong Lead**   One thing that can be tricky about single jumps is having to make a flying change upon landing. If the single jump is your first fence on the course and it is headed away from home, the horse will—more often than not—land behind your leg. If you then have to change directions, it can be difficult to change the lead (as opposed to changing after a line when your horse is galloping forward and up to pace; or on the diagonal, when changing leads is easier just by virtue of the line).

    Practice at home over Fence 3. Jump the obstacle. Slow your horse after the fence and change to whatever lead you *didn't* land on. If necessary, do simple changes at first, but make sure you make the change on a straight line. Practice until you are comfortable changing leads after the fence.

STRAIGHT LINES

In a straight line, the jumps are positioned so one perpendicular line goes right through the middle of all of them. Riding straight lines is the easiest way to learn about lines in general. Unless you learn to ride straight lines well, more advanced things such as bending lines or rollbacks will be beyond you.

Under normal circumstances, straight lines include two or three fences. Two-jump lines are less complicated and more appropriate for lower level riders than three-jump lines.

Line construction has no hard and fast rules except that the more jumps there are, the more complicated the line becomes. One line could include four fences (a single jump and a triple combination). In special situations, a line for advanced riders could have five jumps (a triple combination, with a jump into the line, and a jump out of the line). Generally speaking, however, there are usually only two or three jumps in a line.

The number of strides between jumps in a line may vary. In-and-outs and combinations will have no strides, 1 stride, or 2 strides separating them (for more on combinations, see p. 213). A normal line will have 3 or more strides between fences.

Keep the Pace

The only way you can regulate the distance between jumps on a straight line is through pace. In other words, if you jump the first obstacle too strong, the only way you can fix the distance to the second jump is to shorten stride. If you are very short on your landing, the only way you can fix the distance to the next fence is to lengthen stride.

The fewer strides between fences, the more accurate you must be with pace to get your distance. If you are working under the pace on the way to a 1-stride in-and-out, you will miss the distance and come up short. Then your horse will have to make a tremendous effort to make up the distance in the single stride between fences in order to get a good jump out.

The longer the distance between fences in the line, the more time you have to correct an error. If you are under the pace coming into a 5-stride line, you have 5 full strides in front of you to make up for it.

STRAIGHT LINES ···

Up to a point, the more strides there are between fences, the less accuracy is necessary for the line to work. After 6 or 7 strides, however, as the line gets longer, the law of diminishing returns applies. Very long lines are challenging. It is difficult to learn to maintain your pace for a totally even 8 strides. It is much more tempting to speed up or slow down.

When riding long, straight lines with more than seven or eight strides between fences, it is usually best *not* to count strides. At that point, you are better off relying on your eye, your timing, and your feel for distance.

Riding the Two-Jump Line

The key to riding a line well is deciding beforehand how you will ride it. Walk the line whenever possible (see "How to Walk a Distance," and "What You Can Learn" on p. 167). Know how many strides you want to take. Know what pace you want to keep. Then, follow your plan.

Set the pace you think will work and maintain it. Ride the first jump and head straight toward the second. In general, when riding a normal line:

- If you meet the first fence well, change nothing on your way to the second fence.
- If you meet the first jump slow, you need to speed up.
- If you meet the first jump fast, you need to slow down to make the second fence work.

When riding any line, your goal is always to be able to relax and do nothing on the last stride and over the obstacle. In order for that to happen, you must be able to relate the first jump to the second jump.

In other words, if you are on a forward 5-stride line and are working at the right pace, but come to the first fence a little short and end up short on the landing, then what was forward becomes *very* forward. You will have to increase your pace in order to get the right distance to the second fence.

Conversely, if you are on the same 5-stride line and fly over the first fence, what was a forward line might then become a quiet, steady line instead.

● EYEING THE LINE (TWO JUMPS)

Preparation

Use Fence 1 and Fence 2 of your practice course. The fences should be set 72 feet apart, for a normal 5-stride line.

Schooling

1. Establish your pace. On your approach, focus on the highest point in the middle of the first jump.
2. As you start to sense your distance, raise your eyes and look at the highest point in the middle of the second jump. Relax and jump the first fence.
3. Maintain your speed and stay on a straight line.
4. As you see the distance to the second jump, relax. Raise your eye to continue the straight line after the jump.
5. Jump the line from both directions. Always look ahead for the next place that you want your horse to go (figs. 11.11 A & B).

The Point

Working on a simple straight line is great for learning related distances. It teaches you how to make your performance on one jump relate to your performance on the next. It also encourages you to keep your eyes up, look ahead, and pay attention to how the ride feels.

What Can Go Wrong & How to Fix It

- **Going Too Slowly** This is a normal 5-stride line. If you meet the first jump too quietly and don't realize it, the line will ride too long. In order to make the distance to the second fence, you will have to make a big move on the fourth and fifth strides. You will be pushing the horse forward on the last stride—and that's not good. You must have an accurate feel for the horse's home base pace so if you meet the first fence too slowly, you recognize it immediately. That way, you have the whole line ahead of you to get up to speed.

11.11 A *As you jump the first fence, keep the horse straight on your line. Fix your eye on the second fence.*

B *Keep your pace and your line absolutely consistent between fences. Relax over the second fence. Raise your eye and continue on your line.*

STRAIGHT LINES

- **Going Too Quickly**   Working over the pace will cause you to make a "flyer" over the first fence. Upon landing, if you don't immediately make an adjustment, you will realize too late that you don't have enough room. You will have to yank on the horse to fit in the fourth and fifth strides. You will be pulling to slow down on the last stride—and that's also not good. Again, an awareness of your home base pace will allow you to immediately recognize that you are going too fast. Then, you will have 5 full strides ahead of you to rate your horse's speed.

Variations

- Practice your *position.* Ride the two-jump line back and forth until it becomes so easy and natural for you that you can start to focus on particular parts of your position while you ride it. Practice landing with your weight in your heels. Practice holding the arch in your back. Practice keeping your leg in correct position and your hands and arms light. (Later, practice honing these same things while riding the three-jump line.)
- Practice your *releases.* As you become more and more adept at the 5-stride line, and as you are consistently able to relax over the second fence in the line, you can start to perfect a more advanced release over the second jump.
- Play around with *pace.* Ride the two-jump line normally, in 5 strides. Then slow way down and ride it in 6 steady, even strides. Practice adding a stride from both directions. See how the exercise changes, depending on whether you jump the vertical or the oxer first.
- Practice *transitions.* Canter the first part of the line and trot the last part. Trot the first part and canter the last. Canter the first fence; stop; back; then trot out. Transitions from one gait to another on a line of fences will do wonders for getting your horse supple, relaxed, and light for his jumping work.

Start at the End: Strategies for Three (or More) Obstacles

Every jump you add makes a line more complicated. The same principles still apply, however. You just need to be more aware of all the variables.

The key to successfully navigating lines with multiple jumps in them is starting at the end.

For example, let's say that you have a line of two fences that needs to be ridden in a forward 4 strides. If you knew the distance between both fences was slightly long, you would approach the first fence at a faster pace. Then you would maintain the pace down the line between the two fences.

If you add a third fence to beginning of that line, however, your strategy must change. Let's assume that the distance between the first fence and the second fence of the line is now a normal 4 strides, with the forward 4 strides occurring between the second and last obstacle.

You must approach everything about the line with the goal of being able to jump the last fence well. Because the distance from the first fence to the second is set for a normal 4 strides, you will have to ride the approach to the first part of the line at your home base pace.

Land slowing down from the first jump, with your eyes on the second jump. Then, as soon as you see the distance, increase your speed for the second jump.

On the other hand, let's say you were to ride the same three fences from the opposite direction—with the forward 4 strides at the beginning of the line and the normal 4 strides at the end of it. In that case, your plan for the line would focus on being able to slow down for the second jump in order to reach the third one in 4 normal strides.

Remember, everything hinges on the last jump in the line. You have to meet the fence just before it at the right pace in order to make the last jump work.

● EYEING THE LINE (THREE JUMPS)

Preparation

For this exercise, use Fences 6, 7, and 8 on your practice course. The fences are set up 48 feet apart from each other. After allowing for takeoffs and landings, that gives you 3 normal strides between fences.

Keep the jumps low at first. Raising the fences will significantly affect the difficulty of the exercise.

STRAIGHT LINES ···

Schooling (Beginner & Intermediate)

1   Establish your pace. On your approach, raise your eye and look at the highest point in the center of the first vertical.

2   As you see your distance to the first fence, look at the highest point of the oxer. Relax and let the horse clear the first jump.

3   Maintain your pace and line. As you see the distance to the oxer, look at the highest point in the center of the last vertical. Relax and let the horse clear the oxer.

4   As you see the distance to the last fence in the line, raise your eyes to a point at the end of that line to keep yourself on a straight path. Relax and let the horse clear the final fence.

5   Maintain your pace and line on the departure.

6   Practice the three-jump line from both directions. Concentrate on developing a feel for distance while you keep your pace even and your line perfectly straight.

The Point

In this exercise, you have to make your adjustments quickly, efficiently, and with the least amount of change possible. Focus on keeping your pace absolutely consistent while you find the distance to each fence.

What Can Go Wrong & How to Fix It

• **Misjudging Your Distance**   Practice, practice, practice. If you establish your home base pace early and meet the first fence straight, you should clear the jump and be perfectly set up to take the rest of the line in stride—provided your path and pace don't change.

   If, however, you are working under pace, and you chip in and miss the distance to the first fence, then you will have to really push your horse to make the second fence.

   The second jump then leads to the last jump in the line. If you fly over the second fence, the rest of the line will have to be ridden quietly.

11.12 A *If the horse is heavy on your reins, stop him after jumping the first fence in the line.*

B *Back the horse up a few strides before picking up the canter and finishing the line.*

Practice the line from both directions until you are comfortable maintaining your pace so you can take each fence in stride.

- **Losing Your Line**   Use your eyes to keep you on the "straight and narrow." Always keep your focus ahead of you. Never look down at the fence you are jumping.

- **The Horse Is Heavy over the Jumps or on the Lines**   If you feel like your horse is "lugging" on the reins, or is doing the exercise on autopilot, mix things up a bit to help keep him light. Surprise him. Jump the first fence into the line. Stop. Back up. Then, pick up your canter and jump out. Get him thinking about using his hindquarters for both brakes and impulsion. It will lead to a lighter, more responsive front end (figs. 11.12 A & B).

JUMPING FROM A TURN

A very common piece of a course involves making a turn and jumping a fence or a line of fences.

My pet peeve about jumping off a turn is when people make "square" turns. This happens when the rider goes from one straight line to a second straight line and tries to connect them as if the lines are at right angles, making a square corner. Even if it were possible for a horse to make a square turn, you would have to slow your pace too much.

The correct turn is the curved line that allows you to go from one straight line to the next without changing your pace.

Your goal when jumping a fence off a turn is to keep the curve of your line smooth. The horse should be nicely bent, without cutting in or bulging out. Your pace should remain consistent, without speeding up or slowing down over the fence (fig. 11.13).

The best exercise I have found for learning to judge distance and pace when jumping off a turn, is one you are already familiar with (see "One Jump on a Circle," p. 165). Practicing on a circle allows you to perfect your pace and your path while maintaining an "endless" turn.

Bear in mind that your speed is relative to the turn. The tighter the turn, the slower you go. The wider the turn, the more you can increase your gallop, or pace.

11.13 Keeping the horse straight on a turn means keeping his body on a steady, consistent arc—no cutting in and no bulging out.

ANGLED JUMPS

Often, a line or the placement of a jump requires that you ride an obstacle on an angle.

Angling a fence means that you maintain a straight line on the approach to the jump, across the jump, and on the landing of the jump. The line itself does not bend or have an angle in it. Though the line stays straight, it meets the jump at a slight angle instead of perpendicularly (fig. 11.14).

What's the Angle?

Jumping a fence at an angle can help you slightly alter the distance after the jump and use it to your advantage.

11.14 *"Angling" the jump: the rider guides the horse on a straight line that meets the fence at an angle.*

More often than not, the angled fence is used to create a straighter line between two jumps. It allows you to either take fewer strides, or take the same number of strides with lessened pace.

For instance, if you have two fences on a bending or broken line with a forward distance, taking the first jump at an angle can allow you to ride a straighter line between the two jumps, which can make the forward pace more comfortable.

In addition, if you have a tight turn after a jump, you could opt to angle your approach. Taking the jump at an angle could make the tight turn after landing a little bit easier.

● THE ANGLED FENCE

Preparation

Start with Fence 3 and Fence 4 of your practice course. Keep the fences low at first, so you can concentrate on the exercise.

ANGLED JUMPS

Schooling

1 Jump the vertical (Fence 3) as a single angled jump. Jump it from both directions, on both angles.

2 Jump the oxer (Fence 4) as a single angled jump. Jump it from both directions, angling both ways.

3 Practice a variety of angled fences. Practice with cross-rails, verticals, and oxers. Practice on both leads, toward home, away from home, toward the rail, and away from the rail. Practice jumping every fence in your home course at an angle.

The Point

Dream up different angles and different approaches to your lines. See how taking one fence at an angle affects your distance to the next fence in the line.

This exercise is useful for improving your eyes and your steering. It is also a simple way to introduce you and your horse to the concept of jumping a fence without heading straight toward it.

What Can Go Wrong & How to Fix It

• **Jumping Off-Center**   Jumping a fence at an angle does not mean that you should sacrifice correct placement. Pay attention to your line. Focus ahead of the fence, along a path that will bring your horse over the middle of the obstacle.

• **The Horse Chips the Fence**   This is a common problem, especially for timid or less aggressive riders. If the horse consistently adds a short little stride before taking the angled fence, you are not riding him toward the fence with enough pace. Establish the faster pace well before you begin your approach to the fence and the chipping should stop.

• **The Horse Is Confused or Surprised**   Some horses are initially unsure about jumping angled fences. Use your legs and opening reins to consistently guide and direct him straight on the line you have chosen.

BENDING (OR BROKEN) LINES

A bending line may follow a straight or a curved path between fences. It may also change direction, arcing from left to right.

A bending line may have two or three jumps in it. As with straight lines, two jumps in a bending line are easier to ride than three jumps, but the premise remains the same.

On the bending line you do not always ride in a straight path from the center of one jump to the center of another jump. You also don't necessarily jump each fence with the horse facing it head-on.

Generally speaking, your starting point involves an approach on a straight line that allows you to be perpendicular to the center of one obstacle as you jump over it. You then follow a curve, or arc, that brings you perpendicular to the second jump in the series so you can jump its center. Your departure continues the line of your jump straight away.

However, you may choose to ride less of a curve from one fence to another. You may also jump one or more fences in a line at an angle in order make the distance between fences ride better or reduce your time (fig. 11.15). As you can see, bending lines introduce many variables.

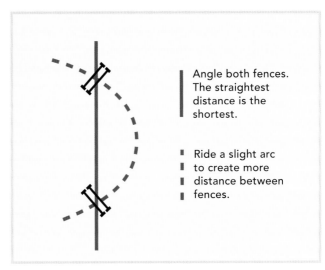

11.15 *Path options of a bending line.*

Path + Pace = Distance

While straight lines rely solely on pace to regulate the distance between fences, bending lines offer many more options. The further out you go along the curve, the longer the distance you will have to cover. In the same vein, the straighter the line, the less distance you have between obstacles.

Let's say that you have a bending line that is exactly 72 feet on a curve from the center of a vertical to the center of an oxer. If you jump the vertical on a straight line and then make a gentle curve at an even pace to the center of the oxer, you should be able to do the bending line in 5 normal strides.

BENDING (OR BROKEN) LINES

Strategies for Bending Distances

If you have a horse that is *short-strided*, you can do several things to present him in a better light. For instance:

- If the line curves to the left, you could go a little left of center on both jumps. You would still face the fences head-on, but you wouldn't jump them from the exact center. This would make the distance from fence to fence slightly shorter, though the curve remains the same.
- You could also choose to angle across both jumps rather than facing each fence on the perpendicular. In this option, you would still jump the center of each obstacle, but the line that connects the two centers would be straighter, and therefore shorter.

If you have a *long-striding* horse on the same exercise:

- You would do best to go wide on your curved line to give him a little more distance and let him shine.
- Since, in our example, the line curves to the left, you might want to jump each fence a little right of center, to give your horse a more gradual, but longer, curve between the two.

● THE TWO-JUMP BENDING LINE

Preparation

Steps 1–6: Use Fence 3 and Fence 4 of your practice course. The centers of the fences should be set 84 feet apart, allowing you to follow a normal six stride bending line.

Steps 7–11: Use Fences 4 and 5 from your practice course. Walk the line before jumping it and determine the best path for even, normal strides.

Schooling (Beginner & Intermediate)

1 Use the vertical (Fence 3) for your first fence. Find a straight approach and establish your pace.
2 As soon as you see your distance to the fence, relax and raise your eyes to the center of the oxer (Fence 4).

3   Pay attention to your pace. If you are on your home base pace, follow an easy arc to the oxer. If you are slightly under pace, make a more direct approach. If you are slightly over pace, widen the curve a bit.

4   Jump the oxer (Fence 4) and maintain the new line through your departure.

11.16 A *Approach the first fence on a straight line. As you jump the fence, look ahead and begin your curve to the second jump. Use just enough hand to guide the horse on your curve without interrupting his jump or follow-through.*

B *Continue the curve to the second jump. Use your rein to guide the horse. Use your leg to keep a bend in his body.*

C *In the air over the second fence. Though you ride on a curve between fences, you should arrive at the second jump in a straight line. Use your hands and legs to keep the horse straight.*

5   Practice the exercise until you can reach the oxer in *exactly* 6 even strides, even if you are slightly under or slightly over your home base pace (figs. 11.16 A–C).

6   When you are comfortable taking the fences from one direction, ride the same exercise from the other direction.

BENDING (OR BROKEN) LINES ···

Schooling (Intermediate & Advanced)

7   Make a straight approach to one oxer (Fence 4). Maintain your pace and your line until you see the distance to the fence.

8   Raise your eye to the center of the next oxer (Fence 5). Relax and jump the first fence.

9   Maintain your pace as you follow a curving path to the second fence. Adjust your path, rather than your pace, to get the correct distance.

10 Jump the oxer (Fence 5) and maintain your new line through the departure.

11 Practice the exercise until you can ride the bending line from either direction in *exactly* even strides, even if you are slightly over or slightly under your home base pace (figs. 11.17 A–C).

11.17 A *Keep the horse absolutely straight on your line over Fence 4, but raise your eye and plan your path to the next jump.*

B *Focus on Fence 5 as you bend the horse around the curve.*

C *As you see your distance to Fence 5, guide your horse on a straight line over it.*

The Point

This exercise is an excellent way to learn to use different paths to connect two fences. It also reinforces the concept of using pace to help you with distance.

Remember: if you ride the first fence at a strong, forward pace, you will have to arc more and follow more of a curve in order to make your distance to the second fence. If you ride the first fence more slowly, your line to the second fence will have to be straighter and more direct.

What Can Go Wrong & How to Fix It

- **Not Learning from Past Mistakes**   Stay consistent until you find what works. For instance, maintain the same pace throughout the exercise, but change your line to make that pace work. Or, keep the line constant and experiment with pace to find one that works.
- **Choosing the Wrong Pace or the Wrong Line**   Riding a bending line is an acquired skill. You learn it by doing it. The key is to approach the first fence on a straight, consistent line and pace. As you see the distance, keep the pace and softly redirect the line to the second fence.
- **Overtaxing the Horse**   When you practice bending lines, remember to keep the fences low or use rails on the ground until you have a good grasp of how to ride the exercise. Low fences are just as effective as higher ones to teach you how pace and path affect distance.

Straightening Out the Bend

Your familiarity with angled fences (see "Angled Jumps," p. 195) can be an invaluable help to you when negotiating bending lines.

● THE ANGLED LINE

Preparation

Beginner and Intermediate Work: Use Fences 3 and 4 of your practice course.
Advanced Practice: Use Fences 4 and 5 from your practice course.

Walk the straightest line possible between both fences before jumping them and determine the best pace for even, normal strides.

BENDING (OR BROKEN) LINES··

Schooling (Beginner)

1 Jump Fence 4 perpendicular, meeting it head-on.
2 Continue in a straight line toward Fence 3. Maintain an even pace.
3 Keep your line straight. Jump Fence 3 at an angle.
4 Repeat the exercise.

Schooling (Intermediate)

1 Jump Fence 3 at an angle, heading toward the oxer (Fence 4).
2 Maintain your pace as you head in a straight line toward Fence 4 (figs. 11.18 A & B).
3 Jump Fence 4 facing it head-on, perpendicular to it.
4 Repeat the exercise.

11.18 A *Approaching the first jump in the line at an angle. I have seen my distance and have raised my eyes to the next fence. The horse is straight as an arrow. We will hold our line across the jump.*

B *Landing on the line after taking the angled fence. We are headed straight to the rails of the oxer (Fence 4) ahead.*

Schooling (Advanced)

1 Jump Fence 4 at an angle away from home. Continue on pace in a straight line to Fence 5.

2 When you find your distance, relax. Raise your eyes to follow a straight line after the fence. Jump Fence 5 at an angle.

3 Repeat the exercise. Get comfortable with the pace you need to make the line straight and take both fences at an angle (figs. 11.19 A & B).

4 Practice the exercise from the other direction, beginning with jumping Fence 5 at an angle and following a straight line to jump Fence 4 at an angle.

11.19 A *Just before taking off over Fence 4 at an angle, raise your eye and look straight ahead at the next fence in the line.*

B *Ride a straight line between fences, then take Fence 5 at an angle.*

BENDING (OR BROKEN) LINES ·······················

The Point

Throughout all your angle work, concentrate on the line you want to follow over the fence. Establish your pace first. Then find and follow your line. Once you find both pace and line, don't deviate until you have landed on the other side of the jump.

What Can Go Wrong & How to Fix It

- **Trying to Do Too Much, Too Soon**   When working on beginner and intermediate lessons, jump only the vertical (Fence 3) at an angle. Plot a straight line so you jump the oxer (Fence 4) head-on.
- **Weaving Back and Forth on the Approach**   The shortest, easiest way to get from Point A to Point B is in a straight line. If your horse constantly needs redirecting, you are probably not using your eyes correctly. Look *ahead* of your next fence. Know where you want to go. Have a clear, definite path that you want to take. Then steer your horse straight along that path.
- **Oversteering or Micromanaging the Horse**   Beware of relying too much on the reins in an attempt to force the horse along a particular path. Keep your eyes up, looking at the highest point of your next jump. Use your reins and legs to keep the horse straight and to maintain his pace. Then leave him alone. Allow him to carry you forward and do his job.
- **The Horse Veers Off the Line**   Use your eyes to find and follow the path ahead of you so you can instantly sense when your horse will be coming off the line (fig. 11.20). Use your opening reins and your legs to guide the horse straight on the line you have chosen to follow.
- **Changing Leads before the Fence**   Sometimes the horse will change his lead just before jumping an angled fence. This is not a big problem. The best way to deal with it is to not worry about it. Instead, focus on keeping your line straight.
- **Swerving to One Side after the Jump**   When training, always do the opposite of what the horse is inclined to do. For example, if you are practicing an angled jump and your horse adamantly swerves to the right afterward, plan on turning left. Approach the jump head-on. As your horse

11.20 *If you wait until the horse veers off the line, it is too late to correct him. Use your eyes and plan your path so you can immediately tell if the horse is thinking of going astray.*

comes off the ground, turn your head and look left. As you land, turn the horse left. Do this until the horse is comfortable turning left after the fence. Then, ride to the jump on the angle. Look straight ahead at the line in front of you. Relax a little bit and the horse will hold himself straight.

More Fences; More Planning

A three-jump bending line is difficult simply because you must string several pieces together into a whole.

In the three-jump broken line, path and pace determine your distance just as they do for two jumps in a broken line. But the exercise hinges on how you want to ride your last fence. Here's why:

Let's assume you are doing a line that curves first to the left and then to the right, with 5 normal strides between fences. If you go too wide on the curve from the first fence to the second, you will end up jumping the second jump on a line that angles away differently than you had planned. This will cause you to follow a path that makes your curve to the third jump wider than intended, which will, in turn, significantly change the distance or affect the number of strides to the third jump.

BENDING (OR BROKEN) LINES··

So, once again, the trick is to figure out how you want to jump the second fence in order to get a good third jump. Once you know that, you will see what you have to do with the first jump.

Let's say you decide that the best way to ride the second and third fences involves jumping the second obstacle on an angle in order to take a straighter path between the fences. This decision will directly affect how you plan your ride from the first fence to the second in order to meet the second fence at the correct angle. The end of the line affects the beginning.

Let's Talk about Leads

In a bending line, a change of direction indicates a change of leads. So many riders see a broken line on a course and spend all of their energy obsessing about the lead change. It's not worth it.

Do not worry about leads on this exercise. I can't stress this enough. Your horse will either change leads…or he won't. It doesn't matter.

If your horse does automatic lead changes, ride nice, big, sweeping curves. He will make the changes, his strides will be even, and the distances will work out.

If your horse doesn't do the flying change, ride the line so he doesn't have to. Angle your jumps to give him the straightest track possible down the middle, so the lead he is on doesn't make a difference.

Furthermore, if your horse doesn't change leads well, practicing broken lines with large, arcing, generous loops between fences can work wonders for teaching him how to.

● THE "S" CURVE

Preparation

Use Fences 4, 5, and 9 of your practice course (fig. 11.21).

To make things a little simpler at first, you may wish to replace the rails of Fence 9 and change it from a skinny fence to one of normal length.

Walk both lines before jumping them and determine the best path for even, normal strides.

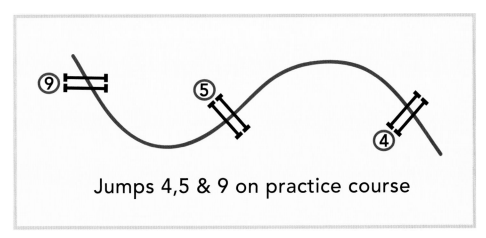

Jumps 4,5 & 9 on practice course

11.21 *The "'S' Curve" exercise.*

Schooling

1 Since you are already familiar with Fence 4 as the first fence of a bending line (see "The Two-Jump Bending Line," p. 198), use that oxer as your first fence in this exercise. Establish your pace. Make a straight approach to the fence. Maintain your pace and your line until you find your distance.

2 Raise your eye to the center of the next oxer (Fence 5). Relax and jump the fence.

3 Maintain your pace as you follow a curving path to Fence 5. Adjust your path, rather than your pace, to get the correct distance.

4 As you see your distance, raise your eye, turn your head, and look to the center of the next fence (Fence 9). Relax and jump Fence 5.

5 Maintain your pace as you follow a curving line to Fence 9. Adjust your path as necessary to get the correct distance.

6 Jump the last fence (Fence 9) and maintain your new line through the departure.

7 Practice the exercise until you can ride the bending line from either direction in *exactly* even strides. Practice riding it "extra bendy," or "extra straight." Practice riding it fast, slow, long, and short. See how different approaches, different paces, and different lines affect your horse's distance.

BENDING (OR BROKEN) LINES ···

The Point

Because of the change of direction in the middle of this exercise, it is an excellent way to supple your horse and get him relaxed and responsive from left to right.

Riding an "S" curve is a great way to gain independent control of your hands and eyes. You should start to understand the intimate connection between looking where you want to go and feeling the distance to a jump. You should also develop an awareness of how different paths affect your pace and the number of strides between jumps.

The bending line will hone your ability to stay with the horse's motion instead of getting ahead of him, falling behind, or leaning to one side or the other. Throughout the exercise, you must stay centered on the horse. Your hands and legs are the guiding aids, rather than your body.

What Can Go Wrong & How to Fix It

- **Your Line Is Wrong or Your Pace Is Off**   Expect this at first. Anytime you ride broken lines, you have to be ready to make an adjustment in either the number of strides or in your line. It is not an exact science. This is why broken lines are more advanced exercises. It is also why more variations are acceptable in broken lines than in straight lines. The more you practice this exercise, the more you will see how pace affects it. Practice until you can readily see how differing paces on differing paths between fences affect your distance.
- **Riding a Section Too Slowly**   As soon as you realize that you are meeting a jump too quietly, make your line more direct to compensate for the short distance.
- **Riding a Section Too Quickly**   As soon as you realize that you are meeting a jump too fast, take the obstacle and let the horse land carrying you. Rather than slamming on the brakes to fit in the preplanned number of strides, you can choose to stay wide and let your line help you to correct the distance to the second jump.

END JUMPS

An end jump is easy enough to identify—it is a jump located at the end of the ring. An end jump makes an extra "line" on your course, requiring you to plan for an obstacle positioned along the width, rather than the length, of the arena.

Since you almost always approach an end jump off a turn, it presents several options. You can opt to stay to the inside of the line, straighten out the path between jumps and ride what might be normal strides. Or you can stay out, ride a wider turn and add a stride before taking the end jump.

Without an end jump on a course, you would normally have time to regroup and refocus when riding the width of the ring. But, an end jump changes all that. End jumps come up fast. They require advance planning to jump them successfully.

The best exercise I have found for learning how to negotiate end jumps is to use three jumps on a circle.

● THREE VERTICALS ON A CIRCLE

Preparation

Steps 1–3: Use Fences 2, 9, and 6 of your practice course. Make sure that Fence 9 is centered between Fences 2 and 6. Remove all fill from Fences 2 and 6, leaving just the standards, with nothing between them. Set Fence 9 very low.

Steps 4–6: Use a ground pole, cross-rails, or low vertical pole to add fill to Fence 2 to make a simple, low vertical fence or cross-rails. Continue using Fence 9 from Steps 1–3.

Steps 7–8: Use a ground pole, cross-rails, or low vertical pole to add fill to Fence 6. Continue using Fences 2 and 9 from Steps 1–6.

I rarely use oxers for this exercise. Never set up more than three jumps on a circle. Be sure all fences are low and can be jumped from either direction (fig. 11.22).

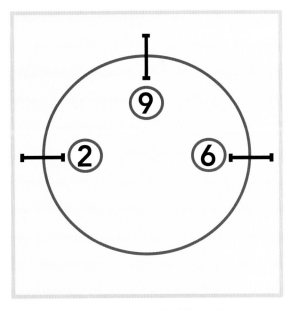

11.22 *The "Three Jumps on a Circle" exercise.*

END JUMPS

Schooling (Beginner)

1 Keep your heels down and start cantering. Canter all the way around the circle.

2 Look at the center of your fence throughout your approach. As you see your distance, raise your eye and look past the jump on your circle. Relax over the fence.

3 As you land, turn your head and continue to look around the circle until you find the fence again. Continue for several rounds. Practice the circle from both directions.

Schooling (Intermediate)

4 Canter the circle.

5 Look at the center of your fence as you approach it. Drift a bit to the inside or the outside of the circle in order to make your distance. When you see it, raise your eyes and look at the next fence.

6 Continue circling, looking ahead to each jump as you see the distance to the one in front of you. Practice the circle from both directions (figs. 11.23 A & B).

Schooling (Advanced)

7 Canter the fences in a circle. Continually look ahead to the next fence as you find your distance to the one in front of you.

8 Continue circling. Practice the exercise from both directions.

Variations

• Adjust to a slower pace, but stay on the same path as you add a stride to each fence.

• Adjust to a wider path that brings you to the outer edge of the jumps, but keep your pace and add a stride to each fence.

• Adjust to a straighter path between two of the jumps, but keep your pace and subtract a stride between fences.

11.23 A *As he clears one jump, the horse doesn't know what's coming next. Everything about the rider must clearly indicate the direction.*

B *The horse is on a beautiful curve as he lands from the first jump and follows the rider's guidance to the next fence.*

The Point

This exercise will help you gain confidence jumping a fence that is placed "width-wise" in the ring. It is a great way to get your mind off the difficulty of jumping an end jump. Instead, you simply practice finding the center of each jump while staying on a nice curve that allows you to get from one obstacle to the next.

This exercise has the added benefit of developing your understanding of pace and line as well. Every fence you jump on a circle is a jump off a turn, or a jump on a bending line. The circle just gives you a simple, controlled way to practice.

END JUMPS

What Can Go Wrong & How to Fix It

- **Becoming Confused or Frustrated**   This exercise can quickly become complicated. If you find yourself getting anxious or upset during any part of it, stop. Relax. Go back and reacquaint yourself with your home base pace on a 5-stride line (see "Finding 'Home Base,'" p. 160). Find what is comfortable, normally, for both your horse and you. Then go back and try the exercise again.

- **Missing a Distance or a Fence**   Remember that experience is the best teacher. The more times, and the more different ways you do the exercise, the better you will be able to understand it and work with it. When you miss a distance or a fence, learn from it. Apply what you have learned and continue the exercise.

- **Throwing the Horse's Head Away**   Maintain light contact with the horse for the intermediate and advanced portions of this exercise. You won't have time to jump with a long release and then regain your contact in time to curve around to the next jump.

COMBINATIONS AND IN-AND-OUTS

Combinations and in-and-outs are a very good way to learn about pace. They are also a good way to teach your horse to be careful and to use himself effectively.

Whether the combination has two or three fences, and whether the distance between fences is 1 stride, 2 strides, or no strides, the principles of navigating the obstacle are consistent.

As with straight lines, the more distance within the in-and-out, the less accuracy you need to successfully negotiate it: 2 strides are easier than 1 stride, which is easier than no strides.

Ordinarily, if different types of fences are used within a combination, the first element is a vertical and the second is an oxer. If the first element is an oxer and the second is a vertical, the level of difficulty increases.

If you are new to in-and-outs (or if your horse is), or if you are uncomfortable with them, it is best to start with a 2-stride obstacle. That way, even if you get "in" wrong, you have two strides to recover before you have to get "out."

Pace is the primary regulator in combinations and in-and-outs. Since the fences are so close together, there is very little you can do with the line.

Always try to do the correct number of strides within a combination. If you misjudge the jump "in" so badly that you can't get out in the right number of strides, your horse will automatically add a stride to get you "out."

Since the fences for combinations are so close together and almost always occur in straight lines, they are easy to recognize on the course. (You will occasionally see in-and-outs on a curve in an equitation course. This is a very rare, very advanced test for you or your horse.)

All the elements of a combination are considered as one obstacle, though you jump them separately. On the course chart for jumpers and equitation rounds, each element has the same number followed by a letter, such as "7A" and "7B," or "4A," "4B," and "4C." Within hunter courses, each element is considered a separate jump and numbered separately.

In any case, you must jump the fences in order or be disqualified. If, for some reason, you stop in the middle of a combination, you must rejump all of the elements in the correct order.

COMBINATIONS AND IN-AND-OUTS

11.24 *The "bounce." The horse is landing from the red "in" and preparing to take off over the yellow "out." The rider's job is to stay with the motion and not interrupt the jump at all.*

Like the rest of your course, in-and-outs and triple combinations are based on a horse's normal 12-foot stride.

- A *"bounce,"* or *no stride* in-and-out is two fences set 12 feet apart, allotting 6 feet for the landing of the first fence and another 6 feet for the takeoff for the second. The horse jumps in, lands, gathers himself, and jumps out (fig. 11.24).
- A *1-stride* in-and-out is two fences placed 24 feet apart, allowing for a 6-foot landing, one 12-foot stride, and a 6-foot takeoff.
- A *2-stride* in-and-out has 36 feet between fences.

Creative Uses for Combinations

Though in-and-outs are set up for cantering or galloping strides, they can also make great *schooling gymnastics*. For example:

- Trot the approach to a normal 2-stride in-and-out. Land in the canter. Add a stride between fences to jump out after 3 strides.
- You can do the same exercise with a 1-stride in-and-out. Trot "in," land at the canter, take 2 strides and jump out.

Combinations are also great ways to perfect your *feel for pace.*

Once you and your horse are comfortable with the fences set for a normal 12-foot stride, then you can get a little creative with the distance between fences. Remember, anytime you change your distance, you must also change your pace.

- You can make the distances a little shorter. Then, you would need to work a little slower, and your horse would have to collect his stride in order to make a nice jump in, as well as out.
- You can also lengthen the in-and-out to get comfortable increasing your pace and working with a slightly longer distance.

● IN-AND-OUT

Preparation

Use Fences 7 and 8 of your practice course. Remove the fill from Fence 6.

Move the standards for Fence 8 closer to Fence 7, so that 36 feet separate the two. Drop the rails to make each element very low at first (fig. 11.25).

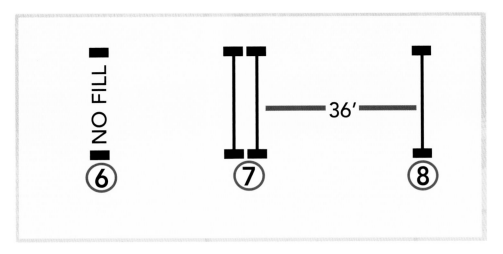

11.25 *The "In-and-Out" exercise.*

Schooling

1 Establish your pace well before the first element. Look at the highest part in the center of the first fence as you begin a long, straight approach.

2 When you find your distance, raise your eye to the center of the second fence. Relax and jump "in." Maintain your line and your pace *exactly*.

3 Raise your eye and follow your line past the second fence. Relax and jump "out."

4 Continue your line through your departure.

5 Practice the 2-stride in-and-out until you are comfortable with it and can jump it from both directions.

COMBINATIONS AND IN-AND-OUTS ....

Variations

- Set up the obstacle so that each element is 24 feet apart for a 1-stride exercise.
- Set up the obstacle so that each element is 12 feet apart for a no-stride exercise.

The Point

In order to get comfortable with in-and-outs, you need to jump them a lot. If you are unfamiliar with them, it is a good idea to include them as a regular part of your practice course.

What Can Go Wrong & How to Fix It

- **Getting in Wrong**   This is the hardest thing about in-and-outs. It is what scares people. If you have a particularly bad jump into the combination, it is difficult to get out in the correct number of strides. If you are not confident about finding your way "in" well, be sure to keep the jumps low and inviting enough that you can get "out" without shattering either your own confidence or the confidence of the horse. The more familiar you are with how in-and-outs feel, the less concerned you will be about navigating them.
- **Weaving, or Veering Off the Line**   Use your eyes to find your line. Use your hands and legs to keep the horse straight.
- **Clutching at the Horse**   As soon as you see the distance to the first element, relax and let your horse do his job. At first, use a long release, hang on, and go along for the ride. Once you know how the exercise should feel, you can start to keep more contact through the jumps.

● A WINNING COMBINATION

Preparation

For this exercise, use Fences 6, 7, and 8 of your practice course. Move Fence 8 so it is 12 feet closer to Fence 7—they will now be a total of 36 feet apart. Move

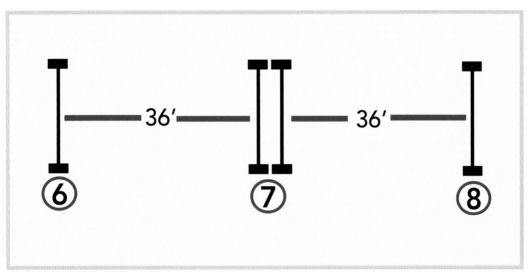

11.26 *A triple combination exercise.*

Fence 6 the same distance toward Fence 7 so they are a total of 36 feet apart. The result should be three elements, each 36 feet apart from the other in a perfectly straight line (fig. 11.26).

Drop the rails to make each element very low at first.

Schooling

1 Establish your pace early. Find your line of approach as if you were going to jump a line beginning with Fence 6. Raise your eye and look at the highest part of the combination's first element.

2 Throughout the combination, when you see your distance to one fence, raise your eye to the highest part of the next fence.

3 Maintain your pace and your line. Relax as the horse jumps each element.

4 Keep your eyes up, your pace consistent, and your line straight through your departure from the third element of the combination.

5 Practice until you are comfortable with the triple combination from both directions.

COMBINATIONS AND IN-AND-OUTS ·······························

The Point

Home is the best place to practice what will be expected of you in the ring. In-and-outs and combinations are some of the easiest pieces to assemble at home because they change very little in appearance when you encounter them in competition.

What Can Go Wrong & How to Fix It

- **Loss of Pace**   This exercise hinges on your horse maintaining a 12-foot stride throughout the combination. Know your home base pace. Establish it early and make yourself keep it through all three elements.
- **Losing the Line**   Raising your eyes and looking ahead of you is critical. This exercise will quickly show you if you are allowing your eyes to roam.

ROLLBACKS

Rollbacks are commonly found in one form or another on everything from equitation courses, to hunter rounds, to jump-offs. On a rollback, you jump one jump, make a "U-turn," and jump back in the opposite direction over a different jump (fig. 11.27).

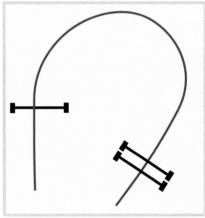

11.27 *The rollback.*

You will usually be asked to jump into one line, turn out of the line, and roll back to a jump on a different line. This can manifest itself on the course in several ways:

You may jump one jump on a straight line and roll back to a jump on a diagonal line.

You may jump a fence on a diagonal line and roll back to a jump on a straight line.

On occasion, you will be asked to roll back from a jump on one diagonal line to a jump on a different diagonal line.

Rollbacks are, essentially, two jumps on a turn. In theory, the better you are, the shorter and tighter you can make the rollback. If you know that you and your horse are good at rollbacks, you can show off a little bit and make as short a turn as possible without losing accuracy.

Slow-Rollers

As you come off the first fence and get ready for your rollback, remember to keep your line on your landing. Look straight ahead. Land straight and start to slow down.

When you approach the turn, turn your head to look at the next jump. As you slow down on your original line, look back and find your new line. Then make the rollback toward the next jump so you end up jumping it straight.

The trick is to *slow down* going into the turn and continue working forward in a slow pace through the turn (fig. 11.28). That makes it possible for you to either wait or move up and increase your pace off the turn, as necessary.

If you are late bringing your horse back, you may end up making your turn too wide and losing your line to the next fence. Otherwise, you will be slowing down off the turn, which will compromise your distance.

ROLLBACKS

11.28 Your speed is proportionate to the turn. In other words, the tighter the turn, the slower you go. The slower you go, the more impulsion you need.

As you slow your horse going into the turn, be sure that he continues to work forward and stays in front of your leg. Then, when you feel your distance to the next fence, your horse is already forward and able to re-establish his home base pace.

● ON A ROLL

Preparation

Use Fences 1 and 4 of your practice course. (Fences 2 and 5 would also work well.)

Schooling

1 Establish your home base pace. Approach Fence 1 on a straight line, as if you were going to do Fences 1 and 2 on a 5-stride line.

2 Stay straight over Fence 1. Ride straight away on your departure, but slow the horse down.

3 Look over your right shoulder, around the turn you will make, and fix your eye on the highest part of the center of Fence 4.

4 Slow your horse enough to make a controlled turn to the right. Keep your legs on him to help him maintain his impulsion, regardless of his pace.

5 Set the horse on a straight line over Fence 4. Bring him back up to pace on the approach.

6 As you see your distance to Fence 4, relax. Raise your eyes and look beyond the fence in a straight line.

7 Jump Fence 4. Maintain your line straight away from Fence 4 on your landing (figs. 11.29 A–D).

8 Practice rollbacks from both directions. When turning to the right, you will jump Fence 1 and then Fence 4. When turning left, you will take Fence 4 first, and then Fence 1.

11.29 A *Look straight ahead as you jump Fence 1. Begin softly bringing the horse back.*

B *Settle into your saddle and slow the horse down as you go into the turn. Look for the next jump.*

C *Stay with the horse's motion as you negotiate the turn. Keep your eyes on Fence 4.*

D *Takeoff for the final fence of the rollback should be straight and clean. (Note the location of Fence 1, visible behind the oxer.)*

ROLLBACKS

Variation

- If using Fences 2 and 5 for this exercise, jump Fence 2 and head in a straight line toward Fence 1. Then, slow down and roll back to jump Fence 5.

The Point

The rollback is one of the best possible exercises for teaching you the importance of keeping the horse in front of your legs and maintaining his impulsion even when decreasing his speed.

It is also an excellent way to perfect your eyes and your balance, and quickly teaches you to plan ahead.

What Can Go Wrong & How to Fix It

- **Missing Your Line**   Consistent, strong, accurate use of your eyes is essential to staying on track in a rollback. Concentrate on using your eyes. Ride straight over the first jump. On the landing, ride straight while you slow down and look at the next jump. After making the turn, as you see the distance for the second jump, raise your eye and either look straight ahead or look for your next jump (if it is on a turn).
- **Rushing the Turn**   This will cause you to make a wide, sweeping turn, instead of a nice, tight one. Not only will it look sloppy and uncontrolled, but it will also make it difficult to find a straight line of approach to the second fence of the rollback.
- **Going Too Slowly**   If you opt to take the short rollback turn to the oxer, you have to go slow because it's a short turn. But, while you are going slowly, you have to maintain impulsion, or make sure your horse is carrying you more and more forward. If you crawl through the turn, your horse will "fall behind" you. Then you won't have enough impulsion, or enough horse in front of you, to get across the second jump.
- **The Horse Falls behind You**   If pace is not at fault, and your horse still consistently falls behind your leg, ride the rollback in three-point position. Keep your angles closed, but put your seat into the saddle. Use your leg and your seat to help keep the horse in front of you while you collect his stride.

- **Slowing Down Too Late**   Slow down first, then make the turn. If you slow down too late, you will be pulling on the horse as you come off the turn and head back to the second fence. This can also result in putting the horse behind your legs, which means that your driving aids lose their effectiveness and your horse loses impulsion. Then you can't get the horse up to pace in time to make the fence off the turn.

  Remember to slow down as you ride the straight line after your first fence. Turn your head to look at your next fence. Don't speed up as you make the turn, but continue to keep the horse in front of your legs so when you ask him to move out, he can.

WALKING AND TROTTING JUMPS

Sometimes, to test the horse's willingness and responsiveness, or the rider's control, you may be asked to walk or trot a jump. Walking or trotting an obstacle removes the element of timing that comes with cantering or galloping. But, *not* cantering to a jump has its own challenges.

Walkers

You will rarely, if ever, be required to literally walk over a jump on a course. However, you may be asked to approach an obstacle at a walk and not begin the trot or canter until you jump the fence.

Walking approaches to fences test the horse's athleticism and compliance. They are not always found on courses, but you shouldn't worry if you encounter one at a show.

When practicing walking to a fence, the lower you can start, the better. A ground pole between standards works well. Give your horse every opportunity to understand what you want and to succeed.

The "cluck" is your key to teaching your horse how to take a walk jump.

Walk toward the ground pole. When you get to the rail, cluck to the horse and lightly use your stick to get off the ground (figs. 11.30 A–C).

After a few times, raise the jump a little bit. Again, walk to the jump. When you get there, cluck and use your stick.

Then, raise the jump a bit more. At this point, when you get to the jump, the horse is probably anticipating the cluck and the stick. Wait. Use just your cluck, and see how he takes the jump.

It doesn't take long before a horse looks at walking jump and thinks, "cluck."

If the horse gets excited or uptight as he approaches the walk jump, anticipate that and make him wait. Soon he will learn that he has to carry you, but he must first wait for instructions.

Trotters

The most important thing about trotting jumps is maintaining an *even pace*. The pace should be as predictable and consistent as a metronome. The more even the pace, the more consistent and smooth the jump will be.

11.30 A *Approaching the walk jump. Throughout the exercise, the horse's ears should be up, he should move in a lively fashion, and carry you nicely.*

B *The takeoff point for the walk jump. Put the reins in one hand, so you can use the stick with the other. Use the stick behind your leg and "cluck" at the same time. Eyes remain up, looking where you are going.*

C *Jumping from a walk. Stay with the horse's motion. Bring the stick back to the reins upon landing.*

WALKING AND TROTTING JUMPS

To trot a fence, your horse should move at a working, or posting trot. The position you post in is exactly the position you use when you jump. Approach the trot jump at a posting trot with your hip angles closed.

Once you have established your trot, the horse should maintain that pace. Throughout the exercise, he should remain on contact. You want him pulling just a little bit so your hands regulate his pace. This means he will be in front of your legs, easily carrying you forward.

As you approach your fence, wait for the horse to take one last short step— the only step that is uneven—and then hop over the jump (figs. 11.31 A–C).

Your horse's job while you are keeping him in the trot is to watch the jump and figure out how he will get over it. If you make him wait, and if you can wait for his last step to be a short one, chances are he will give you a good jump. The arc over the fence will be symmetrical. The line of approach and departure will be even. The horse will land balanced, cantering away from the fence, rather than picking up a canter before you ask him to.

Trotting jumps well is all about practicing them at home. Start low. Use poles on the ground, low jumps, verticals, oxers, spooky jumps, and more difficult jumps. Remember, simply using different types and different sizes of jumps allows you to easily change the exercise's degree of difficulty.

● TROT A ROUND

Preparation

In the beginning, keep all fences of the course low.

Schooling

Trot the course, or trot various parts of the course. Use your eyes to find your lines and help you plan your turns. Focus on keeping the trot absolutely consistent from start to finish. Make up a course, or practice parts of the course. Use your imagination:

- Practice trotting single fences and lines.
- Trot into a line and canter out.

11.31 A *The last step before the trot jump is a short one. Stay in balance with the horse and do not interfere. Wait for the horse to sort out his jump.*

B *In the air over the trot jump. Keep your weight in your heels and maintain a nice line to the horse's mouth.*

C *Canter away from the trot jump. Keep the horse moving forward and look to the next obstacle.*

WALKING AND TROTTING JUMPS ·······························

- Trot into a line, land at a canter, and trot out.
- Trot a fence, or a series of fences, on a circle.
- Canter into a line and trot out.

The Point

Trotting a fence well depends on the rider establishing an absolutely consistent pace and maintaining light contact with the horse. Like everything else, the only way you will get comfortable with trotting jumps is to do them.

What Can Go Wrong & How to Fix It

- **Trying to Time the Jump** Too often, people try to time the trot jump and their horses end up cantering the last step. Concentrate on the trot, not on the distance.
- **Cantering Just before the Fence** If the horse is really having difficulty trotting the entire jump, put a rail on the ground. Walk the rail on the ground until he is comfortable stepping over the rail like any other stride. Then trot over the rail back and forth until the horse is comfortable trotting it. Then make it into a low trot jump and you should be able to regulate the last stride.
- **Stopping, Balking, or Refusing** The moment the horse stops, cluck and use your stick. If he makes a habit of stopping, cluck a few strides before the jump. Remember, your job is to keep the horse moving forward at an even trot. Don't let him change his pace and don't let him stop. Keep the trot. Let him learn to figure out the jump.
- **Getting Left Behind** Trot jumps in two-point position so you are already leaning forward with your hip angles closed and your seat a little bit out of the saddle. Hold on to the mane if you need to at first so you don't get thrown back when your horse clears the jump.
- **Losing Contact** Contact is how you regulate the horse's pace. If you throw his head away, you cannot maintain an even pace. Keep light, steady contact with the horse's mouth throughout all your trotting work.

INVISIBLE JUMPS

This exercise is my specialty—my "secret weapon." It is one of my all-time
favorites. Riding a course without any jumps forces you to look where you are
going. It immediately shows where you are rushing or hanging back, and helps
you instantly identify any problems you may have with pace (figs. 11.32 A & B).

11.32 A *Approach the invisible jump at your home base pace.*   B *Maintain your position and pace as you pass through
the standards.*

● THE "NO-JUMP" COURSE

Preparation

The No-Jump Course consists of jump standards with the fill removed. Remove
all the poles, all the brush, all the ground lines, all the walls, all the gates… everything. Leave only the jump standards with open space between them.

Schooling

1   Pick one pace. Ride the course in its entirety. Ride the pattern as if the
   jumps were still there. You can even ride the courtesy circles, if you like.
   Do not change your pace, no matter what.
2   When you have ridden the course from one direction, begin with the last
   "fence" and ride the elements of the course in reverse order.

INVISIBLE JUMPS ....

3   If a particular jump or line of jumps gives you difficulty, concentrate on it. Ride it back and forth, again and again. Do not change your pace.

4   Continue until you feel totally comfortable and can do the entire course with absolutely no change in pace anywhere on it.

5   Add a jump here and there. Put the fill back in one obstacle at a time. Ride through two or three "jumps" with just the standards up. Keep your pace the same as you take a single low jump with the rails and fill back in place. Then ride through two or three more "jumps" with the just standards up.

The Point

Without having to worry about timing (since there are no fences to meet at a particular distance), you can concentrate on keeping the horse in front of you, carrying you in an even, steady pace.

What Can Go Wrong & How to Fix It

- **Rushing the "Fences"**   Practice the problem obstacle or line over and over. Pay attention to your attitude as you approach the "fence." What signals are you giving the horse that might cause him to speed up? Try riding the entire course a few times in three-point, rather than two-point position. Focus on your position and your horse's pace. There should not be any change in his stride or in his speed when passing a standard that marks a "fence."

- **Inconsistent Pace**   If it is difficult to maintain a consistent pace through the No-Jump Course, do not be in a hurry to put the fill in (Step 5). You might spend several practice sessions progressing through each of the steps until you are ready to add a real fence to the exercise.

- **Slowing Down**   While being unable to maintain a consistent pace generally results from a lack of practice or experience, habitually riding under pace often stems from the rider's anxiety or mental fear.

The No-Jump Course gives the rider a chance to focus on only one thing without the anxiety of timing being a factor.

Even leaving ground-rails between standards is not as effective an exercise, because the rails still require the horse to regulate his stride and find a correct distance to them. Placing rails on the ground can help solve a rider's physical fear of falling off over a fence and hurting himself, but it doesn't solve the mental fear of making a mistake. Mental fear is often the underlying cause that makes riders pull their horses up short and make bad jumping judgments.

Practice the No-Jump Course as often as necessary. Know the distances of your lines, and practice until you can ride at a pace that gives you the correct number of strides between "fences." You may want to focus on Step 3, and just ride a single line until you can do it at the right pace. Practice is your key to consistency.

SAMPLE COURSES

Mastering the various parts of your practice course will give you a wealth of skills to draw from when you encounter a "real course" in competition. You only need to recognize the various parts you have practiced when they show up on the course chart.

To give you an idea of how to apply the hard work you do at home, here are three typical courses: an equitation pattern, an Amateur Owner Hunter round, and a jumper course. An explanation of which skills each part of the course tests follows, with references to the exercise you did at home to learn that skill.

Equitation Course

The equitation course tests the rider's abilities (fig. 11.33).
- The first line is a three-jump line, including Fences 1, 2, and 3.
  From Fence 1 to Fence 2 is a straight line.
  From Fence 2 to Fence 3 is a broken line to an end jump.
- Fence 4 is a single jump, followed by a rollback turn in front of jump 9 to 5A and B, which is an in-and-out.
- Going around the end jump (Fence 3) brings you to the next line–a three-jump line including Fences 6, 7, and 8.
  From Fence 6 to Fence 7 is a straight line.
  From Fence 7 to Fence 8 is a broken line.
- A short rollback turn brings you to Fence 9.
- The course ends with another short rollback turn to Fence 10. You have the option of either going around or in front of Fence 7.

Hunter Course

Hunter courses are designed to showcase the horse's talents (fig. 11.34).
- The course starts with a two-jump straight line from Fence 1 to Fence 2.
- Next you have a long approach to an in-and-out (Fences 3 and 4).
- A simple hunter broken line from Fence 5 to Fence 6 follows.
- The course finishes with a two-jump straight line toward home from Fence 7 to Fence 8.

Jumper Course

Courses for jumpers are constructed to test both speed and agility (fig. 11.35).

- Start with the broken line of Fence 1 to Fence 2.
- Next is another broken line, from Fence 3 to the triple combination (Fences 4A, 4B, and 4C).
- A three-jump line follows with Fences 5, 6, and 7.
  Fence 5 to Fence 6 is a straight line.
  Fence 6 to Fence 7 is a broken line to an end jump.
- The last line is another three-jump line, including Fences 8, 9A, and 9B.
  Fence 8 to Fence 9A is a straight line.
  The course ends with the in-and-out of Fences 9A and 9B.

In the end, it's all about riding your horse *well*.

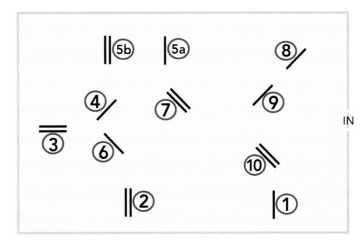

11.33 *A typical Hunt Seat Equitation pattern.*

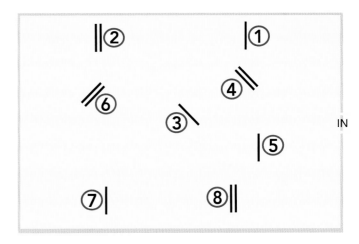

11.34 *A typical Amateur Owner Hunter course.*

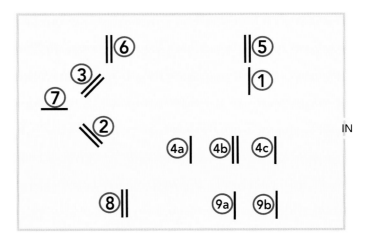

11.35 *A typical jumper round.*

12

Notes for Riding Instructors

The Instructor's Responsibilities

So often, I find that people just breeze over the responsibilities that come with instruction. There are so many who claim to train horses or riders, but who don't take their responsibilities seriously.

We have become a passive society. Few people are really engaged in anything. Often, the result of education is that we produce students who wait for someone else to do what needs to be done instead of trying to figure out how to do things for themselves.

The effective riding program features exercises that force students to figure things out on their own. Find ways to give responsibility to your students so they are not spoon-fed. Your students can learn only if they are part of the process. Encourage active participants. For instance, ask your students to tell you what happened after an exercise. Answering ensures involvement on their part.

Most of my teaching involves setting up different experiences. Since I believe that experience is the best teacher, my responsibility as a teacher is to provide as many experiences as possible.

As far as your teaching is concerned, competence, safety and obedience, empathy, consistency, and fairness are key. Consciously work to develop these attributes in yourself and in your students. Remember: the riding instructor's job is to create the best rider possible—in spite of the student.

12.1 *The instructor's job is to orchestrate safe, effective, engaging experiences. Here, I am helping my student cross her irons properly for work in a riding lesson.*

12.2 Competence means controlling your riding lessons. It means constructing lessons with both the horses' and the riders' safety in mind. In group lessons such as this one, it is not only safe, but it is also good discipline to work on regulating and controlling spacing, keeping one to two horse's lengths between students.

Competence

Competence is a huge component of the riding instructor's responsibilities (fig. 12.2). Don't claim to be able to do something you can't. Continually hone your riding and teaching skills. Be able to demonstrate the exercises you use for instruction. Take lessons yourself. Attend clinics and symposiums. Constantly look for ways to simplify or strengthen your skills.

Competence has to do with having students mounted properly, having the horses tacked correctly and well-schooled, and being sure that you are not asking too much of either your students or their horses.

Don't be embarrassed if a student asks a question you can't answer. Instead, challenge yourself to find the answer. The only shame is ignorance masquerading as egotism.

Safety and Obedience

Safety and obedience are interrelated and are absolutely critical.

Safety is the most important factor when teaching riding. I can't stress this enough. The instructor has a responsibility to protect the safety of both horse and rider. This is a big, *big* deal.

Anytime you wonder whether something is safe or unsafe, you have to stop. Back off immediately and don't do the jump or the exercise. The repercussions of having a student do something you are not sure is safe—and having it go wrong—can be devastating.

Obedience in the rider is a key safety issue. It is 100 percent necessary. A good riding instructor should teach with a dictator's mindset.

I often describe my teaching approach as dictatorial. As far as my students and my horses are concerned, I am in charge. During the course of the lesson, I tend to rule with an iron hand.

If I tell a student to do something and he doesn't do it, I immediately take him down a peg or two. If I say to a rider, "Turn left," "Turn right," "Jump off," or "Go faster," I want to get an instant reaction.

A student of mine was once competing at a horse show. Her horse was very fresh and flying around totally out of control. I knew the horse was going to blow, so I said to the rider, "Get off."

She said, "But, I—"

Then, the horse blew up and she fell off. If she had done exactly what I said when I said it, she would have been fine. She was lucky she wasn't seriously hurt. She learned a valuable lesson that day: listen to the instructor and obey without question.

If I know a rider will immediately listen to me and do what I say, I have a reasonable chance of being able to prevent something from going wrong. I am happy to talk about the situation or discuss it later. But, I don't allow any conversation about what I tell a rider to do. He either does it, or he goes and trains somewhere else.

The more inexperienced the rider, the greater that responsibility is.

As the rider becomes more experienced, more knowledgeable, and better at what he does, part of that knowledge involves him taking more responsibility for his own safety and progress.

Empathy

A riding instructor must have empathy—first for the horse; then for the rider.

Before you teach your very first lesson, commit to doing what is right for the horse and what is right for the rider. When in doubt, what's right for the horse *always* supersedes what is right for the rider.

For example, let's assume a rider wants to jump a 3' 6" course. You know he may be ready, but his horse isn't. So while you can empathize with the rider's desire to challenge himself, you are also aware of the horse's limitations and you don't let the rider do the higher fences.

If the rider gets mad, leaves your instruction and goes to another instructor, the decision is no longer yours to make. Sometimes the rider will leave your instruction, go elsewhere, jump the 3' 6" course and be fine. It doesn't matter. You have to do what you believe is right.

Treat the horses under your care as if they were your own. Commit to treating them ethically, responsibly, and fairly.

Remember, the horse cannot speak up for himself. You must keep the horse's needs in mind at all times. And, very often, you have to protect your students from themselves.

Consistency

The instructor has to take enough time, be creative enough, be interested enough, be strong enough, and be sure enough of himself to make sure that progress happens. Having a clear goal in mind and being consistent and methodical in your approach is the only way to ensure your students' progress.

Let's say I am giving a group lesson on the flat and we're working on "thumbs up."

Throughout the process, I will develop a catch phrase like, "Hands together, just inside the vertical. Thumbs up."

Then I might change the lesson to work on the students' legs. I will talk about leg position and focus on it for a while. But, if I see that a student's hands are falling out of position, I will use the catch phrase.

That should be all it takes.

Then I will go back to work more on the legs. While we work on legs, I will probably come up with a catch phrase to remind the students of proper leg position.

After a while, we might work on distance. And, though we are working on something new, I now have developed two catch phrases to reference what we did earlier. I can consistently remind my students of what they already know without drilling and drilling on hand position for an entire lesson.

In a way, consistency is a sort of brainwashing. Teach the concept. Introduce your catch phrase. Then use the phrase to brainwash the student into good habits.

Fairness

Your riding instruction must be fair, which is not always easy. You must try to be impartial (fig. 12.3).

It is very easy to have favorite students. It is also quite common to have a few students that you really hate to have to deal with. But, take care that your personal feelings do not color the quality of your teaching. Be responsible for keeping your emotions under control.

12.3 Be fair and impartial. Resist the urge to play favorites with your students.

Treating your riders equally does not mean that all riders are equally talented. Nor does it mean that all riders have the same resources, the same support from their families, or the same drive to succeed.

From a businessperson's point of view, however, it is important to be fair to everybody. Teach everyone the same. Give every rider the same opportunities for success.

Barn Management

In all your plans, don't neglect barn management. Your horses' health and soundness supersedes everything.

If you don't take care of your horses and you don't run your stable well, then you don't have anything to work with.

Other Responsibilities

I think it is important that instructors feel a responsibility to their chosen sport. If you have enjoyed a certain degree of success within your riding discipline, I believe it is your right and your duty to give back to that sport (fig. 12.4).

Conducting clinics is one way for teachers to address this responsibility. Get out of your comfort zone. Put yourself on the line and make the information you have acquired available to others.

I challenge equine professionals to be involved in the various organizations

12.4 *Judging is an excellent way to give back to the sport and give others the benefit of your experience.*

of their disciplines, regardless of whether it is at the lowest or the highest levels.

Giving back will not only improve you as an instructor and as a horseperson. It will also strengthen the sport of riding for others, and will allow you to contribute in a very real way.

Student Evaluation

When evaluating a rider's ability, start with the easiest, most basic exercises possible. Often, you will find that most riders can't do them correctly. So then – right at the beginning—you have found something that not only needs work, but is also safe and easy to work on.

The "No Passing" exercise works well to this purpose:

● NO PASSING

When I conduct a clinic (which is essentially a group of new riders that I need to evaluate before I start teaching them), I will often put the group out on the rail and ask them to ride around the ring at one speed.

The riders are to keep their speed consistent and keep their spacing even. They are not allowed to pass the horse in front of them or to change their place on the rail with another.

I have the riders practice this exercise at several gaits, beginning with the walk and the working trot. When they are ready, I have them ride at the sitting trot, the extended trot, and the canter.

I watch how each rider controls his horse. I pay attention to whether or not the rider's seat and hands independently. I look to see how much he relies on the reins for speed control. And I gauge how aware he is of other riders around him.

Most riders have difficulties when first exposed to each exercise. That's fine. I expect it.

Each exercise can help the students immediately identify a weakness and set about fixing it. They can work on something new and interesting. Furthermore, they know they need to work on the exercise, because it is obvious they haven't mastered it.

Do More with Less

When evaluating ability, always ask your students to do less. Set up specific exercises that allow you to easily measure a student's performance. Have him jump a low jump with heels down. Ask him to stop on a straight line. Watch him do a two-jump line.

Analyze the student's mastery of individual "pieces" of riding. In this way, you get the know the rider's strong and weak points. Instead of starting with something advanced and complex and watching the rider crash and burn, it is better to begin with the very simplest exercises.

Use the evaluation exercises to find the weak spots at the very bottom of the rider's foundation. Then build your way up from there.

If you begin with an evaluation of the student's basics, the worst thing that could happen is the student does everything perfectly and you won't find any areas that need work. In that case, you still come out ahead. The end result is simply that the rider feels good about himself—and you know you have covered your bases.

Evaluating the Lesson Horse

Quiet. Reliable. Sound. Comfortable. Knowledgeable. These are all attributes of a good lesson horse.

I also add "orthodox" to the list. The ideal lesson horse is as "normal" a horse as possible. He doesn't have weird idiosyncrasies in his gaits, his training, or his mannerisms. In a perfect world, the lesson horse is honest and straight-forward.

The horse needs to be quiet enough that the rider is not intimidated. It is the instructor's job to set up a situation where the rider can concentrate on his riding instead of focusing on the horse.

Knowledge and training are essential. The less the rider knows, the more the horse has to. That proportion changes as the rider's experience and expertise progresses.

Size is also a consideration. The horse and rider must "fit." If you have a small person, a small horse is better if you can get away with it. Sometimes one must compromise on the size issue. For instance, I would rather have a small rider mounted on a big horse with a good temperament than on a small horse with a bad attitude.

Undermounting is the key. You always want to have a horse that is *too easy* for your students to ride. The horse should be *too* well trained. He should be *too* easily controlled. Riding the horse should be physically and mentally easy for the student. The rider must be able to concentrate on himself and not worry about the horse.

The more of a beginner your student is, the easier the horse he needs to have. As your students progress, you can mount them on more and more difficult horses.

Regardless of the rider's abilities, you are always looking for the best horse. Any success in the show ring is based on mounting your students as well as possible.

I always say that the person who has the best horse wins the most. That is not only true in the Equitation divisions. That is true for every riding discipline, be it hunters, jumpers, dressage, or pleasure riding. The "best" is not always the most expensive—though good horses don't come cheaply. The best horse is one that is better at his job than he needs to be. Then, your students can worry about perfecting themselves rather than correcting training faults.

Teaching Considerations

The instructor's job is to create comfortable, confident, secure riders. This involves giving students a good foundation, spending time, doing exercises to build their confidence, and exposing them to the most positive experiences where they will thrive and succeed. It involves creating experiences that the rider can learn from, and being fair, interested, creative, energetic, and sympathetic.

Developing longevity in a rider's career is a worthy goal for instructors. Ideally, an instructor should produce riders who continue to ride and who go on to train other riders who carry on the tradition of good horsemanship.

Stupid, versus Nervous and Stupid

If you have a horse that is very spooky or very uncomfortable in a certain situation and you really get after him, the only thing you do is add nervousness to his problems.

For example, if you have a horse that spooks at an arched wall because he is afraid of it, beating him to make him jump it will only result in a nervous, stupid horse.

Instead of beating on him, you need to figure out a way to increase that horse's confidence in the situation. Calmly expose him to the obstacle to settle his nerves. Show it to him and clearly communicate what you want without making him nervous.

You are better off with a stupid horse than with a nervous, stupid horse.

You can apply the same concept to the rider. If you have a student who doesn't understand what is happening, who is not able to do what you want him to do, and who is frustrated because of that—if you get after him, you will only make him more upset, and get nowhere.

Often, when the student is starting to get flustered and uptight, it is best to just stop. Think for a moment. Determine what specific piece you are trying to teach. Then, set out to find the best way to get the rider to understand the lesson.

Take a Time Out

When a student is having trouble with a particular point, often the instructor's first inclination is to scream and holler and throw dirt and carry on. Since that is rarely productive, make yourself stop and give some serious thought to what's going on when a problem arises.

Ask yourself, "What's happening? What is the problem? What are the symptoms? What can I do to solve the problem and slow the process down?"

When a student does not understand a concept, it is better to take a step back rather than rushing forward. Stop. Think. Don't just react to the situation. Take the time to make some conscious choices for the good of the student and the horse.

12.5 *Total concentration in every lesson is critical to success. This rider's work ethic is obvious— even when schooling, her concentration and dedication are apparent.*

The Rider's Time Line

It is critical for students to realize that they will not quickly master either the physical or the mental muscles required for great riding (fig. 12.5).

The rider's time line is a long one. It is comprised of many skills learned in small but steady increments.

Because of the nature of the sport, perfection remains a worthy, but elusive, goal. Every great advance in a student's abilities only serves to highlight how much more may be learned.

Every worthwhile instructor should realize that great riders are not made in a month, or in a year, or even in two years. That is why it is so important that you don't overtax your students. If you push so hard that riding is no longer a joy for them, they will quit—and they may never realize their full potential.

Opportunities for Advancement

Knowing when a student is ready to move from one division to another can be tricky. When in doubt, follow your instincts. If you are not sure whether or not a student is ready to advance—he isn't.

A sure sign that the student is ready to advance is when he consistently performs well in his current division and is starting to get a little bored at his current level.

Push your students. But, rather than pushing them to ride faster or jump higher before they are ready, encourage them to explore all the possibilities available.

I like to stretch my students consistently. At some point in nearly every lesson, I will go off on a little bit of a tangent and introduce something new.

Challenging your students requires advance planning. Prepare the arena with schooling fences ahead of time. Set up your lessons so they lend themselves to several kinds of exercises. That way, when the students are ready to practice something new, you can smoothly segue into it. If you are working on going forward, for instance, and the students are doing well, take a break for a while and work on something steady.

Once steadiness is under control, you might want to work on turns to the left. When the left is good, work on something to the right, or a broken line, or a straight line.

Don't drill and drill on the same exercise indefinitely. It will only serve to make your students, their horses—and *you*—irritable and sour. Mix things up. Work on one type of exercise, or one piece of the puzzle. When the students exhibit some new degree of mastery, go on to tackle another piece.

Fix Flaws; Stretch Strengths

Allow your students to tell you what piece they need to work on. Examine their riding. Find the flaws that consistently crop up. Devise an exercise that targets one weak area. Work on that area until you see some improvement. Then, move on to something else for a while.

By the same token, if you ask a student to do a certain exercise and he does it well the first time, then that is the moment to stretch him in that area. Instead of immediately jumping to another piece of riding and working on strengthening a flaw, use the opportunity to build on a strength. You might make the same exercise a little more challenging. Or, you might introduce an exercise that is in the same family, but is a little more complicated.

Stretch—Don't Break

Always remember, you are trying to *stretch* and not *break*.

When stretching, do your best to set the scene for success. If you think a student can do something fairly well, take that chance and challenge him. Make sure the student understands exactly what you want from him. Make sure he knows exactly what the exercise entails. Then, hold your breath and assume you were right—that he was ready, and the exercise will work.

If you suspect a particular "stretching exercise" over fences may be too difficult, lower the jumps. But, remember to set the scene for stretching.

For instance, I believe in setting schooling jumps at the height required for a given division. At the beginning of the lesson, I take a certain number of the jumps down and make them into cross-rails. I temporarily lower the jumps to give the student a feel for the exercise.

If the student gets comfortable with the exercise and does it well at the lower height, then I am in a position to quickly raise the jump to the right height. The same exercise will continue to stretch the student.

Move your students up slowly so they don't have a chance to backslide. Also, cultivate a great knowledge of—and respect for—fear. If fear is involved, your rider won't progress as he should.

Be careful to make the exercises too easy at first. Spend a lot of time building a foundation and building confidence. Only such a foundation will allow your students to progress.

Secrets of Success

As the instructor, you set the tone. The way you approach the sport of riding, the emphasis you place on showing and sportsmanship, your attitude toward hard work and the value that you place on your horses will invariably affect your students. So much of your students' success is directly related to you.

Showing for Success

When you are teaching, it is important to have a clear understanding that showing and lessons are completely different.

If it is the day before the horse show, I want my students just warming up, reviewing, familiarizing themselves with the location, bolstering their confidence, and getting ready for the competition ahead of them.

The show ring is not a place to teach. It is a place to quickly review one or two things that you need to practice to get comfortable and confident, but it is not a time to introduce your students to new things.

In the old days, we used to schedule training breaks from showing to be at home. We would use the time off for lessons and consciously slow down and get back to basics. We would look at the details, figure out what we wanted to improve and work on one piece at a time.

These days, because we show so much, it becomes increasingly difficult to schedule large quantities of "downtime." But, make a conscious effort to pick moments during show season where you have your students go back and review the basics.

In many parts of the country, the show season now lasts twelve months a year. Many professional instructors are being sucked into the idea of using the show ring as a teaching tool. I don't agree with that practice. It is not good for the horses or for the students.

Be sure that you understand the difference between showing and teaching. Make a conscious plan to schedule your year, your show season—even your week—around those two different activities. Include time for both.

More Scheduling Concerns

When scheduling your year, freshness and soundness are the most important factors. Anything you do that involves teaching riding, training horses, or showing horses has to be worked out around a schedule that allows the horses to continue to be sound and fresh and ready to give their best when it counts (fig. 12.6). I credit George Morris for teaching me this ironclad truism years ago.

If you are getting ready for a major event, whether it is the Hunt Seat Equitation Finals, the indoor hunter shows, or the Olympic Games, you need to schedule everything around having sound, fresh horses so they can perform their best when it really counts.

If you have horses that are sore or sour, you students won't be competitive. So do your best to plan your schedule with soundness and freshness foremost in your mind.

12.6 *Plan so your horses arrive at an event sound, fresh, and ready to go.*

On the Road versus Home Sweet Home

When you are on the road, your focus should be on getting the results you want at horse shows. When you are at home, allow some time to get your horses rested. Then, go back and stress the basics in both the horse's training and the rider's.

Whenever possible, break your year down into either competing times or recuperating times. The more clearly the different times are delineated, the better you can focus on what you are doing.

In other words, if you have scheduled time to be on the road and competing, then you must do whatever you can (within reason) to make sure that you have the most success possible. The more successful you are, the sooner you can stop. The sooner you can stop, the sooner you can freshen up your horses, go back and review the basics, and do the teaching and the training necessary to become even *more* successful when you go back out on the road again.

Like everything else in life, there is a balance that must be maintained. Rest often enough that your horses are sound and fresh and your students are motivated. But, you need to teach and train enough so your horses and riders know their jobs and will be successful when you are out on the road.

Learning, teaching, and training are about trying new things and acquiring new skills. Competing and being on the road are about having good habits and being as successful as possible.

Stretch for Success

Each show season, schedule several easy "comfort shows" where your students are able to compete and be successful. In essence, choose a few shows that are beneath your students where they can be competitive and rise to the top.

Then, stretch yourself and go to a bigger or better horse show. At the "stretching shows," your students may not win big. They may not win at all. But, they will be exposed to better jumps, a better environment, stronger competition, and better judging. You will also be able to compare your teaching methods with a higher caliber of trainers. Stretch yourself as well as your students.

Use the stretching shows to help in your goal-setting. Once your students have gotten a taste of competing at a higher level, go back and work until they are as comfortable at the new level as they were before at the lower level. Then stretch from there.

The Speed of Success

A good way to help your students prepare for a successful show experience is to increase their speed when schooling.

When at home, it helps to do everything *over* the ideal pace. If you want a student to be able to ride a course at 14 miles per hour at a horse show, get him comfortable riding at 16 miles per hour at home. Then, the student will be able to slow down at the show without ruining his ride.

This approach is far more effective than allowing the student to ride at 12 miles per hour at home and fool himself into building a false sense of security. That only sets him up for failure when you try to push him up to a more competitive pace at the show.

Doing Your Homework

The same philosophy applies to jump height. Have students get comfortable jumping a bit higher at home than they will be expected to jump in competition. Then, when it counts, the jumps will look a little easier and the students can concentrate on fine-tuning their ride.

In the same vein, make the courses a tiny bit more difficult at home than what your students will be expected to navigate at a show.

If your students have practiced in a small ring at home and then go to a horse show with a big, beautiful ring, jumping the course will be a little bit easier for them. If you know they will have to ride in an open field at the show, find a bigger field at home to practice in so they know what to expect.

Identify what external aspects of a show make your students uncomfortable. Then practice those elements at home in a controlled way.

Stretch your students (and yourself) at home when the pressure is off. That is the secret of being successful at a show. Have your students be comfortable doing a little bit more than they will be expected to do in competition.

Ultimately, I would rather have the horse shows be a showcase for my students' talents than a challenge of their abilities.

Effective Instruction

To be an effective instructor, you must be hyperaware of your students' attitudes and abilities. Above all else, remember to keep safety a top priority.

Experience is the Best Teacher

Never underestimate the need for the students to have many good, positive experiences. As the teacher, you are not *giving* information. Instead, you are setting up situations that *allow* the students to learn from the experience.

Different experiences can include a variety of ring exercises. Allow the students to ride different horses. Let them ride in different bridles and use different bits. Occasionally enter them in different types of classes. Expose them to riding cross-country, riding Western, or doing a little eventing.

Be creative and dream up new challenges. The more different experiences you can arrange, the more thorough you are as a teacher. Any experience you can give to your riders that is safe is a good one. The better those experiences are, the more confident riders you will produce.

So often instruction becomes more about the teacher than about the rider. As teachers, we need to constantly stop and remind ourselves that it is all about the student. It is not about us. We teach people how to ride—that is our job and our responsibility. If we do our jobs really well, our students (not ourselves) will be at the center of attention when they "win big."

Teaching for the Student, Not the Crowd

Teaching the individual student who is part of a group can be very difficult. As the instructor, it is important that you remain focused on one rider at a time without ignoring the group. Tell yourself, "This is my rider. This is what I see. This is what I think he needs to work on." Then, stay focused and do what is best for that student.

It is easy to allow yourself to be distracted when teaching in a crowded schooling area, in a clinic with spectators, or even in a lesson with people watching. Too often, when a student makes a mistake, the riding instructor starts playing to the crowd in the process of correcting it. In such a situation, the instructor tries to make himself look good at the student's expense.

Teaching for the crowd is a very easy trap to fall into. But, train yourself to stay focused on your student. See what is happening at the moment and analyze what you need to do to help each person you instruct.

Lighten Up

Don Stewart, a respected judge and top trainer and rider of numerous "Horses of the Year," once said, "Riding should be serious but not grim." I couldn't agree more.

15 KEY QUALITIES OF EFFECTIVE INSTRUCTION

1 Have a plan. Know where you want your students to go and how you will help them reach their goals.

2 Remain calm and unemotional.

3 Keep it simple. Don't get complicated. Teach one thing at a time.

4 Enjoy yourself and your students will enjoy themselves.

5 Take the time necessary to do a good job in each situation.

6 Be fair.

7 Give each lesson some thought. Carefully consider your answers and consider your questions.

8 Be confident in your abilities. Don't allow yourself to become intimidated. It is very difficult to teach when there are people around, or in a busy area.

9 Develop appropriate catch phrases to make what you teach easier for your students to remember.

10 Develop good, effective exercises. Use a variety of lessons and exercises to teach each concept.

11 Observe carefully. Look for underlying problems rather than just noting symptoms.

12 Explain things clearly.

13 Be able to demonstrate what you are teaching.

14 Stay safe. If you need to change something in a lesson to make it work, take the time to do it. If the bridle isn't adjusted correctly, or if the girth is too loose, or the spurs aren't right, or the jumps are the wrong place—stop. Do what you need to do to get the desired results.

15 Be more interested in your horses and your students than anything else. Do not focus exclusively on yourself. Stay interested in your students' progress, even after they are no longer studying with you.

Humor is a great boon to your teaching. Often you can say something funny and it will help the student to remember the lesson better. It seems that people tend to remember humorous things the best. Humor in teaching is critical.

You can apply the concept to the horse's training as well. If you keep things a little light and breezy with your training, you will have a horse that looks forward to training and responds better than one that is always faced with heavy, severe training and discipline (fig. 12.7).

One Piece at a Time

In order to have a great "whole," mastering the pieces is important.

A big part of teaching correctly is *seeing* correctly. Develop a sense for looking at riders and finding the *one thing* to work on that will make a difference. When that is mastered, then go on to the next thing.

Bear in mind that the student can only concentrate on one thing at a time. The art of teaching involves choosing the correct thing to work on and staying focused on it.

If you have five things that need improving, address one piece at a time.

12.7 *Horses, like humans, are at their best when they don't take themselves too seriously.*

Work on one for a few minutes; then choose something else. Work on that for a few minutes, and then move on to the next item.

Cover pieces in training. Focus on a particular type of jump, or a particular type of line, or a particular type of turn for a while. Practice those pieces as exercises. Get comfortable with them. Then, every now and again (or at the horse shows), string those pieces together.

Appendix

USEF Hunt Seat Equitation Tests

1. Halt (4 to 6 seconds) or halt and back. When riders working collectively are asked to halt and then back, they must not be penalized if they walk forward a few steps and halt after backing.

2. Hand gallop. A hand gallop may be used on the approach to a jump.

3. Figure eight at trot, demonstrating change of diagonals. At left diagonal, rider should be sitting the saddle when left front leg is on the ground; at right diagonal, rider should be sitting the saddle when right front leg is on the ground; when circling clockwise at a trot, rider should be on left diagonal; when circling counterclockwise, rider should be on the right diagonal.

4. Figure eight at canter on correct lead, demonstrating simple change of lead. This is a change whereby the horse is brought back into a walk or trot (either is acceptable unless the judge specifies) and restarted into a canter on the opposite lead. Figures to be commenced in center of two circles so that one change of lead is shown.

5. Work collectively or individually at a walk, trot, or canter.

6. Jump low obstacles at a trot as well as at a canter. The maximum height and spread for a trot jump is 3 feet for horses, 2 feet for ponies in classes restricted to ponies.

7. Question(s) regarding basic horsemanship, tack and equipment, and conformation.

8. Ride without stirrups; riders must be allowed option to cross stirrups.

9. Dismount and mount individually.

10. Turn on the forehand done through the walk or the halt.

11. Figure eight at canter on correct lead, demonstrating flying change of lead.

12. Execute serpentine at a trot and/or canter on correct lead, demonstrating simple or flying changes of lead.

13. Change leads on a line, demonstrating a simple or flying change of lead.

(continues on next page)

14 Change horses. (Note: This test is the equivalent of two tests.)

15 Canter on counter lead. (Note: no more than 12 horses may counter canter at one time.) A canter on the counter lead may be used on the approach to a jump.

16 Turn on the haunches from the walk.

17 Demonstration ride of approximately one minute. Rider must advise judge beforehand what ride he plans to demonstrate.

Glossary

Approach The line leading up to the jump. The approach should follow a pre-planned straight line that leads over the jump and continues without interruption on the other side.

Automatic release The most advanced jumping release. The rider maintains light contact with the horse's mouth off the ground, through the air, and upon landing.

Chipping Trying for a long distance at a fence, missing it and adding a short stride just before takeoff.

Classic equitation (also classic horsemanship) Using time-proven methods to improve one's riding skills.

Conflicting aids Asking the horse to do something with one set of aids, but using another set of aids to keep him from doing what was asked. Sending confusing signals to the horse.

Coordinating aids Using the correct amount of hand and leg together so the horse can understand what to do. Making it clear what the horse is to do, and allowing him to do it.

Course chart A visual representation of the whole course layout, with fences generally numbered in the correct order.

Courtesy circle A circle made at the beginning and end of each jumping round, either bringing the horse up to pace or slowing him down after the course has been completed.

Departure Moving away from a jump. The ideal departure maintains the same line and pace as the horse had over the obstacle.

Dotted line An imaginary boundary, indicated on the course chart with a dotted line, marking the area allotted for a courtesy circle.

Driving aids Aids that encourage the horse's forward motion. These include the legs, seat, the voice (cluck), the stick, and the spur.

Equitation The art of riding the horse. Riding in the most correct, most beautiful, most functional way possible in order to more effectively communicate and influence the horse.

Falling behind What occurs when the driving aids lose their effectiveness and the horse loses impulsion.

Feel A developed awareness of the horse. The perception of touching the horse's mouth through the reins. The ability to identify the horse's individual footfalls and determine which parts of his body are at rest or in motion at any given time. An awareness of the rider's position and of the horse's response to that position.

Forward line A line of fences set up for a longer stride than normal and requiring a faster than normal pace.

Home base pace The speed that allows your horse to negotiate a normal line of fences in the correct number of strides without speeding up or slowing down.

Hunt Seat Equitation A competitive division at horse shows in which the rider, rather than the horse, is judged. Open primarily to riders under the age of eighteen. Developed with the purpose of creating good riders with a strong position and a solid foundation of basic skills.

Independent hands Hands that are light and autonomously balanced on the reins. Hands that can function effectively, without being influenced by what the rider's body does on the horse.

Independent seat The ability to ride in harmony with the horse's movement, using only the leg and base for balance and security on the horse.

Landing Touching down after a jump. The ideal landing follows the same line and is at the same pace as the approach.

Lightness Using the least possible amount of an aid in order to get the desired response.

Long release The most basic jumping release, appropriate for the beginning rider who is learning to jump. The rider moves both hands halfway up the crest of the horse's neck before the jump. The rider pushes down on the crest to stabilize himself over the fence. He may also hold onto the horse's mane for added security.

Mental fear The fear of making mistakes when riding.

Muscle memory When the body is able to maintain a practiced position without needing conscious thought.

Normal line A line of fences set up for a 12-foot stride.

Physical fear The debilitating fear of falling off and hurting oneself when riding.

Primary aid The aid that most directly affects the horse's power and motion.

Resisting the mouth Closing the fingers on the reins and deliberately increasing contact with the horse's mouth in order to correct an unwanted behavior. When the horse relaxes and accepts the correction, the hands instantly relax and reward him.

Secondary aid An aid used in conjunction with a primary aid in order to restrict, redirect, or otherwise fine-tune a maneuver. An aid that protects one aspect of the horse's performance while another aid asks him to do something additional.

Short release A jumping release for intermediate riders. The rider moves his hands about a quarter of the way up the horse's neck from the withers, pressing down on the neck for stability over the jump.

Steady (or slow) line A line of fences set up for a shorter stride than normal and requiring a slower pace than normal.

Takeoff The point just before a jump where the horse pushes off to clear the obstacle. The ideal takeoff is relaxed so the horse can take the jump in stride with no pushing or pulling on the rider's part.

Three-point Riding with three points of contact: both legs and the seat. The rider's body inclines forward at the hips and follows the horse's motion, but the seat remains in the saddle as an additional driving aid.

Two-point Riding with the legs as the only two points of contact between the rider and the horse. Both an exercise and a position for following the horse's motion.

ACKNOWLEDGMENTS

Thank you, Martha Cook at Trafalgar Square, for orchestrating this entire project and making it possible. Special thanks to Caroline Robbins and Rebecca Didier for such conscientious attention to the manuscript throughout the editing process.

Thanks to Diana De Rosa, Miranda Lorraine, the American Hunter Jumper Foundation, Ray Orth, Charles Hilton, and Randy Muster for supplying the beautiful photographs to illustrate the text. Special thanks to Fort Leavenworth Hunt and North Gallway Hunt for the use of their images.

Thank you, Heidi Scheing, for tirelessly tweaking the illustrations until they were perfect.

And, a mountain of thanks to Michele Perla who worked so hard to get the shots we needed.

Thanks from Geoff

I'd like to take the opportunity to thank my mentors.

I was lucky enough to grow up working with a lady named Michael Kelly who was a disciple of Gordon Wright. She had a step-by-step basis for her teaching which she used to prepare people for the hunt field, where I started.

Her methodology was quite unusual. It was very different from the norm for somebody to use a systematic approach to horsemanship just to teach people to ride to hounds.

Michael's daughter Nancy also helped me. I credit her for interesting me in showing in general and equitation in particular.

The next person that I was involved with was Wayne Carroll, who, with his father Frank Carroll, helped me by emphasizing correct riding.

Another major influence was George Morris, who is a law unto himself in American Hunt Seat Equitation. George has helped me in so many ways without even being aware of it himself. Thank you, George, for writing the Foreword.

I credit all of my teachers and mentors for emphasizing correct riding and timeless techniques. In a very real and practical sense, an equitation background prepared me for a lifetime with horses.

Thanks to Joe Fargis for writing the Introduction and for being a great example for all of us.

A world of thanks to Cathy Warner—who runs Montoga—for helping me through both photo shoots.

Thanks so much to all the people who spent so much time and energy posing for the photos. Special thanks to Julia Capalino for getting up at 5 A.M.—even on your "day off."

Thank you Michele Perla, for dropping everything over your 4th of July weekend, traveling to another state, and managing the entire photo session. You knew I couldn't do it on my own and graciously took time out of your busy life to help.

Special thanks to Diana De Rosa, our extraordinary photographer who asked, "Where do you want me and what do you need me to do?" You worked tirelessly for twenty-four hours straight and kept the project on track.

And, thank you Ami Hendrickson, not only for working so hard to get my words right, but also for being a truly great professional, a hard worker, and for maintaining such a great sense of humor. You are amazing.

Thanks from Ami

Thanks to Geoff Teall for being such a gracious host and a wonder to work with. You have so many great ideas and are committed to getting things right. You are a true credit to your horses, your students, and your sport.

Thanks to Diana De Rosa and Michele Perla for working so diligently on the photos at a moment's notice. The book literally would not exist without you.

Thank you, Ray Orth, for sharing your photos from the field. Hats off to you!

Thanks to "Sir Charles" for being so willing to help out.

Thanks to Paula Horsch and Denise Hettig for selflessly reading and commenting on the "understandability" of early drafts.

Thanks, of course, to Robert and Cassandra—my wonderful family. None of this would be worth it if I didn't have you to come home to.

Index